Dr. R. T. Kendall's i[...]
ings have had a sig[...]
thinking. I respect Dr. Kendall greatly and am
honored to call him my friend.

—JAMES DOBSON
FOUNDER, FOCUS ON THE FAMILY

Prayer should be on top of every Christian's
agenda; the Lord's Prayer should be at the top
of their prayer guides; and RT's book may be
placed at the top of simple, clear expositions of
the Lord's Prayer.

—MICHAEL EATON, THD
NAIROBI, KENYA

This will make the Lord's Prayer famous among
a new generation of believers.

—COLIN DYE
PASTOR, KENSINGTON TEMPLE, LONDON

Dr. R. T. Kendall takes the most famous prayer
in the world and illuminates its timeless truths.
It is one thing to recite the prayer; it is quite
another to understand why it should be prayed
today. Let one of the best Bible teachers in the
world show you.

—CANON J. JOHN
EVANGELIST

THE
LORD'S
PRAYER

R.T. KENDALL

publisher nor the author assumes any responsibility for errors or for changes that occur after publication. Further, the publisher does not have any control over and does not assume any responsibility for author or third-party websites or their content.

Visit the author's website at rtkendallministries.com.

Cataloging-in-Publication Data is on file with the Library of Congress.
International Standard Book Number: 978-1-63641-197-2
E-book ISBN: 978-1-63641-198-9

23 24 25 26 27 — 987654321
Printed in the United States of America

Most Charisma Media products are available at special quantity discounts for bulk purchase for sales promotions, premiums, fund-raising, and educational needs. For details, call us at (407) 333-0600 or visit our website at www.charismamedia.com.

To Charlie, Lyndon, and Rob

CONTENTS

THE LORD'S PRAYER

Our Father in heaven, hallowed be your name, your kingdom come, your will be done, on earth as it is in heaven. Give us today our daily bread. And forgive us our debts, as we also have forgiven our debtors. And lead us not into temptation, but deliver us from the evil one.

—Matthew 6:9–13

FOREWORD

WE LIVE IN a world in which communication feels, at times, like a pandemic. Words, ideas, and even emotions move with unstoppable velocity. The human race has honed the science and art of transporting content to one another. But we are, I fear, at the mercy of the medium and are losing our own messages.

A century ago people communicated through a limited number of methods. Primarily we talked to one another. Over the last few decades, all that has changed. Mobile phones, email, social media, and a myriad of instant messaging options have transformed our communication methods. In the current technology, Twitter is one of the most popular forms of communication. To participate, you "tweet" your message for the entire world to read via the internet. But there is one caveat: your message must be fewer than 140 characters. Even with this limitation, many use Twitter as a primary form of communication to give and receive information.

Correspondence is occurring more frequently and at a faster pace, but possibly with an atrophying impact. We dance along a tightrope of increased communication lacking any depth or significance. With such self-imposed limitations placed on our communications to one another, there must be a spiritual consequence. It cannot be denied that in a time when tools for communication are growing more powerful, our ability to relate is weakening. In speaking more rapidly, we are listening less intently.

But by God's blessing, there is an answer to such a predicament. God has endowed us with a form of communication that can be ignored by man but which never loses its power with Him: prayer. It remains the ever-present answer to our communication weakness. It requires no great skill of oratory. Prayer humbles us before God and emboldens us before man. Prayer can be as short as an instant message or as long as a great work of literature. Whether brief or lengthy, God is awaiting our response to His initiatives through prayer.

One of the great lessons we learn about prayer is that, although it is a form of communication between God and His people, it is not merely for communication. Prayer is one of the primary vehicles by which God delivers us into the middle of His plan and purposes. As Jesus taught His disciples, prayer was to show them how to speak and how to listen to the Father. Whereas we live in a world in which it is easy to make one-way declarations, prayer demands a listening ear as well.

In the pages to follow, we will be taught how Jesus' model prayer has withstood earth's time and man's reluctance to reveal God's heart for us to follow His will. Prayer is, after all, not just our opportunity to speak. It is a sacred moment in which to listen as well.

R. T. Kendall has become a trusted friend in my life. Always insightful and always seeking God's power for his life, he presents to us a work on prayer that is worth your time, thought, and investment. Why is it worth it? Because he has lived out its truths before teaching them to us. In *The Lord's Prayer*, R. T. Kendall takes us on a journey through prayer to obedience. By using the Lord's Prayer as the foundation, we will better learn to discern the will of God with a trail guide who has been to the mountaintop many times before.

Pastors often hear the question "How can I know God's will for my life?" Strangely enough, most people who ask the question know that prayer is the starting point. But whether from arrogance or apathy, some believers have left any serious praying in the hands of others. Expecting the professional clergy to do it on their behalf, too many Christians engage in prayer only briefly—when it is offered by their pastors during Sunday services. Meanwhile God stands on the ramparts of heaven, ready to dispatch His power, explain His will, and bring His people into the midst of His activity. But only if we will call upon Him.

God desires for us to ask Him about His will for our lives so we can rightfully receive it. Because He is gracious, He will express His grace toward us, explain His wisdom to us, and reveal His power through us. Many years ago, E. M. Bounds put it best: "God's conquering days are when the saints have given themselves to mightiest prayer."[1]

Books on prayer line the shelves of all types of bookstores. People are fascinated by the possibilities held by prayer. They are curious to see what God will say and what He will do if they pray. But we should expect more from those who teach on the subject of prayer. It is reasonable to expect that they have spoken well to God and have heard well from Him. In R. T. Kendall we have such a person.

As his pastor and friend, I can tell you that R. T. Kendall knows prayer and knows our Lord, so when he writes on the Lord's Prayer, I pay attention. This book will give you fresh insights and encouragement and should be read not just once but multiple times.

I am honored to offer a few of my thoughts on how needy the church is for a fresh work on the subject of prayer. I anticipate that our Lord can use this work by His man to transform the thinking of many Christians. My prayer is that your prayers will grow from the biblical lessons contained in the pages to come. And as your prayers grow, so will your participation in the mission of God's kingdom in our world today.

—ED STETZER
EXECUTIVE DIRECTOR, WHEATON COLLEGE
BILLY GRAHAM CENTER;
DEAN, SCHOOL OF MISSION, MINISTRY, AND
LEADERSHIP, WHEATON COLLEGE;
AUTHOR, *COMPELLED BY LOVE*

SPECIAL
RECOMMENDATION

I HAVE OFTEN WONDERED what kind of prayer John the Baptist taught. "Lord, teach us to pray, just as John taught his disciples" (Luke 11:1). Given his appearance, diet, and public ministry, one might assume John's pattern of prayer might be different from Christ's.

Whatever it was, it could not have been the powerful model of prayer given by Jesus. Brilliant in its economy of language, powerful in its simplicity of design, and transcendent in thought, the Lord's Prayer, so called, is the full, perfect, and sufficient arsenal for the believer's daily prayer.

Dr. Kendall gets us deeply into this great prayer and thereby gets it deeply into us. His insights are profound and his applications practical. As anyone who knows Kendall or has benefited from his ministry might easily have predicted, the heart of the book—the pulsing, quivering, throbbing heart—is the matter of forgiveness, appropriate since that is also the heart of the prayer.

I believe that true genius makes the complicated seem simple. False genius makes the simple seem complicated. The genius of God is in the Lord's Prayer, and the genius of R. T. Kendall has made it reachable, touchable, and doable. That is the genius of this book, for the Lord's Prayer must be *done*, not simply recited. First do this book. Then do the Lord's Prayer.

—MARK RUTLAND, PhD
FOUNDER AND DIRECTOR, NATIONAL INSTITUTE OF
CHRISTIAN LEADERSHIP AND GLOBAL SERVANTS;
AUTHOR, *OF KINGS AND PROPHETS*

SPECIAL RECOMMENDATION

I HAVE KNOWN AND loved R. T. Kendall for four decades now. If ever a book on prayer was born out of a life of prayer it is the one you now hold in your hands. This is not just another theoretical treatise but a book that issues out of a life well lived and immersed in communion with God. Well after we are in heaven, in the presence of Him who taught us to pray, this volume could well be listed among the classics on prayer along with the likes of those by E. M. Bounds and R. A. Torrey.

RT and I do not see "eye to eye" on certain minor points of doctrinal truth and biblical interpretation. However, one thing is rock-solid certain: we are in lockstep agreement that prayer is the battlefield of the Christian life. Some believers get all dressed up with the armor of battle Paul describes in Ephesians. We put on the breastplate of righteousness, the helmet of salvation; we hold the sword of the Spirit firmly in hand and gird ourselves with biblical truth while standing in the shoes of peace. But many believers seem to have no idea of where the battle is actually being fought. After describing this armor, the great prayer-warrior apostle plainly reveals in the very next verse where the battlefield is found: "Praying always with all prayer and supplication in the Spirit." Kendall serves as a field general when it comes to calling the troops to the place of battle.

As the pages of this volume unfold before your eyes and heart, you will be moved to a passionate longing to know Him in the intimacy of Father and child. The Christian world owes a sense of deep gratitude to God for the gift He has given us through R. T. Kendall in this volume on prayer. It will move you, as it did me, to join the disciples in their heartfelt request, "Lord, teach us to pray."

—O. S. HAWKINS
FORMER PASTOR OF FIRST BAPTIST CHURCH, DALLAS
PRESIDENT/CEO, GUIDESTONE FINANCIAL RESOURCES
SOUTHERN BAPTIST CONVENTION

SPECIAL RECOMMENDATION

THROUGHOUT THE AGES those we view as the great saints have all proclaimed prayer to be the secret behind their powerful ministries. These ordinary Christians simply took to heart the teaching of the Bible that exhorts Jesus' disciples to "pray and not give up" (Luke 18:1), be "faithful in prayer" (Rom. 12:12), "keep on praying" (Eph. 6:18), "devote yourselves to prayer" (Col. 4:2), and "pray continually" (1 Thess. 5:17), and they got results.

However much we may envy their success, the fact remains that prayer is as available to us as it was to them. The same God who proved Himself strong for them is willing to be sought by our generation. Prayer is one of the most vital issues facing Christians today. We live in a demanding age. The very speed of life and the pressures of the modern world conspire to overwhelm our spiritual walk. God is looking for individuals who, through prayer, are keen to allow the power of the Spirit to be manifest through them to the world at large. But how do we pray?

Jesus' disciples instinctively knew that they needed to be taught how to pray. They therefore came to Him and simply asked Him to teach them. We too must realize that there is a way to pray effectively—a learning process that all of us need to discover for ourselves. We may have tried before to establish a prayer pattern but with limited success. Though our flesh is weak, we must never forget that our spirits are willing!

The apostle Paul in no way condemns us for our weakness. Instead, he acknowledges it, stating that "we do not know how to pray" (Rom. 8:26, RSV), but adding that the Spirit is there to help us. Without the Spirit's touch, the Lord's Prayer is a mere ritual. But when the Spirit brings its importance to our hearts, it becomes the most dynamic prayer that we can ever offer to the Father.

Few can parallel R. T. Kendall's outstanding ability to make the Scriptures come alive and lead us by the hand into an experience of their power and helpfulness to us. I happily commend this volume to you, knowing you will be greatly blessed if you feed on its truth and take its advice. I want to particularly commend to you RT's extraordinary insight into the issue of forgiveness and its power to release you into ever-increasing effectiveness for God. May this book immediately be put into effect by your transformed experience of the Lord's Prayer.

—TERRY VIRGO
FOUNDER, NEWFRONTIERS

PREFACE

I WAS THRILLED WHEN Charisma House asked to publish my book on the Lord's Prayer. This is taken from my sermons based on the Sermon on the Mount (Matt. 6:9–13).

Strange as it may seem, I did not learn the Lord's Prayer at my church. My old church in Ashland, Kentucky, was an informal Holiness church and rather prided itself on being non-liturgical. They never recited the Lord's Prayer. Nor did we recite it in my home. I had godly parents, and we had regular family devotions. But we never recited the Lord's Prayer. I learned it in the public schools in Ashland from 1941 to 1944. What is so very, very sad: public schools in America no longer recite the Lord's Prayer. It is not even allowed.

As I say in this book, the Lord's Prayer is meant to be prayed today—in church and in private. My wife, Louise, and I have prayed it throughout our marriage for years and years. We pray it out loud together every day.

I pray that this book will be a blessing to you and that your life will be changed.

I want to thank Steve and Joy Strang for allowing me to be a continuing part of Charisma House. I thank Adrienne Gaines and Angie Kiesling for their helpfulness—and especially their patience!

—R. T. KENDALL
NASHVILLE, TENNESSEE
NOVEMBER 2022

INTRODUCTION

This, then, is how you should pray.
—MATTHEW 6:9

I GREW UP IN Kentucky, where it was actually required to recite the Lord's Prayer in the classroom every morning. I now know more than ever how blessed I was as a child. It seems a little strange to say that I learned it not at home or even church but in school. How fortunate that I got in on this before the law in America prohibited saying the Lord's Prayer in public schools.

As I said in the preface, I cannot recall praying the Lord's Prayer at our church services—I suppose they felt doing so was too liturgical. Nor did it seem to occur to us as a family to pray it, although we had devotions together daily.

Why do I say that learning the Lord's Prayer as a child was such a blessing? First, anyone who gets a head start in learning what God ordains is singularly blessed. This is why Israel was so blessed. Jews were given a head start in the things of God. This is why they are said to have an advantage—because they, before all others, have been entrusted with "the very words of God" (Rom. 3:2). Secondly, when we are required to repeat something again and again we naturally memorize it. This is why I myself memorized the Lord's Prayer a long time ago. I am so thankful for this. If you don't know it by heart, perhaps you should consider learning it, because you never know when you may need to recall this prayer.

This book you hold in your hands is about the greatest prayer ever uttered, devised or imagined. It was originally uttered, authored and verbally conceived by Jesus Christ Himself—which is why we call it the Lord's Prayer. I regard it as a high privilege and great honor to write this book, with the intent of examining the Lord's Prayer line by line. I pray it will change your life.

Not every prayer in this world is inspired by the Holy Spirit, including too many of my own prayers. It is possible to ask "amiss" (James 4:3, KJV), or ask "wrongly" when you pray (ESV). Praying wrongly is when we don't pray in God's will, either from wrong motives or ignorance. A prayer prayed outside the will of God may or may not be answered, but the only *guarantee* of answered prayer is to pray in God's will. We know this because God promises to *hear* us when we pray in His will. "This is the confidence we have in approaching God: that if we ask anything according to his will, he hears us" (1 John 5:14).

The difficulty is that we don't always know we are praying perfectly in the will of God. Sometimes God lets us know we are praying in His will: "If we know that he hears us—whatever we ask—we know that we have what we asked of him" (1 John 5:15). But this does not happen all the time. However, when you pray the Lord's Prayer you pray in His will. And yet it does not follow that the prayer will be answered immediately, as in the case of Jesus' high priestly prayer for the unity of the body of Christ (John 17:22).

But is it not a wonderful feeling to know you are praying exactly in God's will? Come with me now as we begin to examine this magnificent prayer.

PART I

FOCUSING ON GOD

CHAPTER 1

THE PERFECT PRAYER

When you pray, say...
—LUKE 11:2

THE LORD'S PRAYER is verbally inspired by the Holy Spirit and therefore perfectly worded. It is a revelation of how we should pray because it mirrors God's will for His people. It cannot be stressed too much that Jesus Himself is the formulator of it—every single word—and if you want to know at least once that you prayed in God's will, the Lord's Prayer is for you.

I would hope that God would certainly *not* answer my prayer when I ask for things outside His will. I cherish the knowledge that Jesus my High Priest and intercessor is seated at God's right hand, putting through to the Father only what is His will. I always want the Lord Jesus to filter my praying and not let wrong requests be passed on to the Father. I therefore want Jesus not only to intercede for me but also to *intercept* my ill-posed requests. Jesus knows what is best for us.

The worst thing that could happen to us is for a wrong request to be put through to the Father and then be answered.

Getting all you want would bring incalculable damage and grief to you. Be thankful for unanswered prayer. It may be a sign of God's favor.

One of the most frightful verses in the Bible is this: "So he gave them what they asked for, but sent a wasting disease among them" (Ps. 106:15; "sent leanness into their soul," KJV). Such happens when God's people persist in asking for what God has clearly shown to be out of His will—and God finally acquiesces, to their sorrow.

There are some lessons for us as we approach the Lord's Prayer. First, there is a kind of praying that does not please God. It is praying that profanes His name and His nature. Second, there is a kind of praying that does more harm than good. This happens when a prayer shows contempt for God's glory and encourages people to do the same thing. Third, there is a kind of praying that doesn't get God's attention: for example, when praying is done to impress others.

We therefore should never want what God is against. God did not want Israel to have a king, for example. "*I* am the LORD, your Holy One, Israel's Creator, your King" (Isa. 43:15, emphasis mine). God Himself was already Israel's king. Samuel warned the people against having a king as other nations had, but they persisted. God said to Samuel, "Listen to them and give them a king" (1 Sam. 8:22). God thus granted their request but sent leanness into their souls. It was a pivotal and bad moment for Israel. The day would come when a prophet would say, "So in my anger I gave you a king, and in my wrath I took him away" (Hos. 13:11).

We should always aim to pray in God's will. Praying the Lord's Prayer is to pray perfectly in His will.

Misusing the Lord's Prayer

We *could*, however, pray the Lord's Prayer with a wrong motive. The NIV translates the Greek word *kakos* (often translated as "sick" or "evil") in James 4:3 as asking with "wrong motives."[1] The truth is, although praying the Lord's Prayer is certainly praying in the will of God, one could use the prayer wrongly. How? By believing that the very praying of the Lord's Prayer is a worthy act in itself that makes you righteous before God merely because you pray the prayer. If we repeatedly pray the Lord's Prayer over and over and over again—thinking that merely praying it counts for righteousness before God and scores points in heaven—I would regard this as praying it with a wrong motive. That is hardly the point of the Lord's Prayer.

You could also misuse this prayer by praying it from the head and not the heart. In other words, repeating the Lord's Prayer from memory and not praying it from your heart of hearts could be much the same as the vain repetition for which Jesus rebuked the Pharisees (Matt. 6:7). The Lord's Prayer should be prayed in faith from the heart. In short, you should *mean what you say* when you utter these words.

To be fair, I suspect we've all used the Lord's Prayer inappropriately at times. I would not want you to read my mind every time I led Westminster Chapel in praying the Lord's Prayer every Sunday morning. I *tried* to pray it from my heart each time, but I know that I didn't always do this. There were times my mind was on the sermon to be preached later on, or I would be distracted by someone in the congregation. When you know the Lord's Prayer so well from memory it is easy to repeat the words without faith or feeling.

Two New Testament Accounts

The Lord's Prayer is mentioned twice in the New Testament. In the Sermon on the Mount (Matt. 5–7) the Lord's Prayer comes in the context of Jesus' telling His disciples how not to pray, as well as how to pray (Matt. 6:9–13). He spoonfeeds them, giving them a prayer to pray—line for line, word for word. The other place the Lord's Prayer is mentioned is when one of His disciples implores Him, "Lord, teach us to pray, just as John taught his disciples" (Luke 11:1). Jesus then gives them virtually the same prayer as before (vv. 2–4).

As I said, we call it the *Lord's* Prayer because Jesus Himself was the author of it and also because it was He who told us to pray it. Some think it should be called the Disciples' Prayer since the Lord Jesus Himself would not need to pray it; we do. Some would point out furthermore that Jesus' high priestly prayer in John 17 deserves the title of the "Lord's Prayer." But we will not be pedantic; the Lord's Prayer is the common title to this magnificent prayer we are given by Jesus, and we should be very, very thankful indeed for it.

Whereas Luke's account of the Lord's Prayer came as a result of Jesus' disciples' request—"Lord, teach us to pray, just as John taught his disciples" (Luke 11:1)—Matthew's account came in the context of Jesus' observations of the way Pharisees prayed. My book is not a scholarly treatise, so I will not highlight the small differences between Luke's account and that which comes in the Sermon on the Mount. The interesting point is that Luke reveals that John the Baptist also taught his disciples to pray. Two of Jesus' own disciples had been followers of John (John 1:35–37). We have no idea what John's prayer was like or where he got it. We do know that Jesus was not threatened by the disciples' request. He merely complied and said, "When you pray, say..."—and gave virtually the same prayer as we have in the Sermon on the Mount.

When to Pray the Lord's Prayer

It is good to pray the Lord's Prayer both publicly and privately. I certainly recommend it publicly. Even if it is sometimes used inappropriately, it still finds its way into one's memory. You never know when you will be glad you have it memorized. Some churches regularly make it a liturgical part of their services. Why not? After all, it was originally addressed to the corporate body of Christ. I realize there are churches that react negatively to anything that smacks of liturgy. Dr. Martyn Lloyd-Jones went so far as to suggest that it is spiritual pride, if not arrogance, to refuse to pray the Lord's Prayer with others. Like it or not, all churches have their own form of liturgy, in any case. I would personally urge every church leader to find a place in a service once a week to insert the Lord's Prayer. It will do no harm and only good.

However, there is a fairly strong hint in Matthew's account that Jesus could have meant for the prayer to be prayed privately and behind closed doors. The context of Jesus' inserting this prayer in the Sermon on the Mount was His caution that we should not be like those who "love to pray standing in the synagogues and on the street corners to be seen by men" (Matt. 6:5). He said that when you pray, "Go into your room, close the door and pray to your Father, who is unseen. Then your Father, who sees what is done in secret, will reward you" (v. 6). He concluded this section by introducing the Lord's Prayer.

I would therefore urge that the Lord's Prayer be prayed with other believers and also that you pray it alone in your quiet times. Include it in your family devotions. Pray it with your roommate. Pray it on your way to work. Pray it at work. Pray it with friends. Pray it at Bible studies. Pray it in small groups. Pray it as often as you feel like it—but do so from your heart.

The Purpose of the Lord's Prayer

Jesus showed us how not to pray (like the hypocrites, who want to be seen by everybody) and how to pray (with believers and behind closed doors). Then He indicated the very reason for praying—namely, to be "heard" and "rewarded" by the Father. Does this surprise you? The purpose of praying is that the Father "will reward you" (Matt. 6:6). God Himself loves to appeal to our self-interest. Hence He encourages us to pray in order to be heard and rewarded, on these conditions: (1) we pray to be seen only by Him and (2) to put forth requests that are in His will.

To put it another way: the aim of prayer is to be *heard* by the Father. This is Hebraic thinking that goes back to the Hebrew word *shema*.[2] Every Jew knows about the prayer called the *Shema*: "Hear, O Israel: The LORD our God, the LORD is one" (Deut. 6:4). *Shema* means both to hear and also to obey. You may have said to your child, "Did you hear me?"—implying they must not have heard because they did not obey. That is the idea with *shema*. When God hears us in the *shema* sense, it means He will obey our request. "Your prayer has been heard," the angel said to Zechariah (Luke

1:13). "If we ask anything according to his will, he hears us" (1 John 5:14). Some thought they were "heard because of their many words" (Matt. 6:7). The aim of prayer, then, is to be heard by the Father.

When we pray the Lord's Prayer we are assured of being *heard* by our heavenly Father. I have been struck by a statement that Dr. Martyn Lloyd-Jones made in this connection. He said, "I have always been comforted by this thought, that whatever I may forget in my own private prayers, as long as I pray the Lord's Prayer I have at any rate covered all the principles. On the condition, of course, that I am not merely mechanically repeating the words, but am really praying from my heart and with my mind and with my whole being."[3]

Why Pray?

Just before introducing this prayer, Jesus added a word: "Your Father knows what you need before you ask him" (Matt. 6:8). It should not surprise us that God knows what we need before we ask Him because He knows everything. Essential to His very character is His omniscience (He is all-wise, all-knowing). "Before a word is on my tongue you know it completely, O LORD" (Ps. 139:4). It may be surprising to some that Jesus would say God knows what we need before we ask Him—and then urge us to pray! But it is thrilling that God would remind us of this just before we pray. Why does He do this? Would not this be a deterrent to praying if God already knows what we have need of and always wants what is best for us? Then why pray?

First, because He invites us—even commands us—to pray. The same God who knows in advance who will be saved equally tells us to preach the gospel to every creature (Mark 16:15). We merely obey Him.

When I was at Westminster Chapel we had our Pilot Light ministry. Twenty or thirty of us were out on the streets of Victoria every Saturday morning within the shadow of Buckingham Palace doing one thing: presenting the gospel to passersby. I urged the Pilot Lights not only to present the gospel but to do all they could to convert them. "Treat each person as though their destiny were in your hands," I urged. And yet all this was done with a theological underpinning, namely, that God knew in advance who would receive the gospel. This made no sense to some people. "If God already knows who will be converted, why try to convert them?" Answer: because God told us to present the gospel to every creature and commands everyone to repent (Acts 17:30). As a matter of fact, Paul stated that God even determined where each person should be *born and live* in order that they should seek God (Acts 17:26–27). It is our job to make sure they hear the gospel.

So in a similar way, the same God who knows the end from the beginning (Isa. 46:10) invites us to pray even though He knows what we need before we ask Him. We are instructing ourselves, not God, when we pray, said Martin Luther.[4] We do not pray with the view of informing God, said John Calvin, but in order that we may arouse ourselves to seek Him.[3] John Wesley said that God does nothing but in answer to prayer.[5] By the way, don't worry about asking God for small things—with God, everything is small. It is we who need to pray, not God, said Michael Eaton.

Second, God, who ordained the end, ordained the means to the end. That means: prayer. "Ask of me, and I will make the nations your inheritance, the ends of the earth your possession" (Ps. 2:8). "So I say to you: Ask and it will be given to you; seek and you will find; knock and the door will be opened to you. For everyone who asks receives; he who seeks finds; and to him who knocks, the door will be opened" (Luke 11:9–10). Jesus told His disciples a parable "to show them that they should always pray and not give up" (Luke 18:1). Granted that prayer is an unfathomable mystery only a fool will refuse to pray. It drives pride away; it brings us to our knees, remembering who God is. For prayer reveals the nature of God—not only His unsearchable wisdom but His sovereignty, what He is pleased to do and not do.

Third, God chooses to honor our obedience. He wants us to obey without having to figure everything out first. It is not unlike Moses, who wanted to see why the burning bush was not consumed. Moses had been looking at this extraordinary sight, a bush that was on fire but did not burn up. Moses said to himself, "I will go over and see this strange sight— why the bush does not burn up" (Exod. 3:3). God told Moses to stop: "Do not come any closer...the place where you are standing is holy ground" (v. 5). So with us. Logic would dictate that since God knows our need and promised to supply it, there is no need to pray. Yet God does not honor our logic but our childlike obedience. "You do not have because you do not ask God" (James 4:2). William Temple, former archbishop of Canterbury, used to say, "When I pray, coincidences happen, and when I don't, they don't."[7]

Fourth, God knows our need but dignifies us by letting our praying make a difference. It is an old truism: *prayer changes things.* Some Christians may object to the idea that prayer has power. I can understand that. Prayer in itself has no power; it is the person whose prayer is applied by the Spirit who makes the difference. And yet God stoops to our weakness, making us feel affirmed. Like a wise, loving parent, God could do a thousand things in our behalf without letting us lift a little finger, but He lets us participate in the divine scheme of things, giving us dignity, joy, and a feeling of being needed. He gives us the privilege of changing things through prayer. We can have a hand in diverting disaster. We can have a hand in moving God's heart, following Jacob's example: "I will not let you go unless you bless me" (Gen. 32:26).

Fifth, God promises to answer prayer. That is good enough reason for me! If God promises to answer prayer, I am going to pray! I cannot guarantee that John Wesley was absolutely right when he said that God "does nothing" but in answer to prayer, but God does not promise to act unless we seek Him first. He wants us involved in all He does. For that reason, to be candid, I pray about everything. *Everything.* "In *all your ways* acknowledge him, and he will make your paths straight" (Prov. 3:6, emphasis mine; or, "he shall direct thy paths," KJV).

"All your ways" means everything. I would say this covers a lot! I pray about a grocery list before I go into town. Louise and I prayed for our cat, Gizmo, when we feared she was dying. I started praying for Billy Graham every day in 1981. I ask God to help me know when to say yes and when to say no, in all that pertains to us. You may be sure I prayed about every sentence I wrote in this book. I take Proverbs 3:6 seriously and literally. This verse means He will act when we pray. It probably also means He won't act until we pray. Why? I reckon it is because God gets our attention this way. As we already observed, it is we who need prayer, not God. Prayer is for us, not Him. He promises to answer prayer that we might spend more time with Him. What is more, He likes our company, as I wrote in *Did You Think to Pray?*

Having said that our heavenly Father knows our need before we ask Him, Jesus proceeded to tell us what to pray; hence the Lord's Prayer.

A Pattern Prayer

What, then, is the point of the Lord's Prayer? Although it is a prayer to be prayed by all of us, it is a pattern prayer. For example, it begins with acknowledging God, worshipping Him, and focusing on His interests. Then come the petitions that pertain to us. This pattern is designed to show that we are not to rush into the presence of God, snap our fingers toward heaven, and expect the angels to jump! We begin with proper worship.

All good praying should, in some way, be consistent with the pattern, order, content, and intent of the Lord's Prayer. It is a prayer to be prayed, but the words of the Lord's Prayer serve also as an outline of appropriate praying. We should see each line of the Lord's Prayer—that is, each petition—as the solid foundation for truly worshipful and selfless praying. Thus, everything we say should be an extension, or filling out, to some degree, of every line in the Lord's Prayer. Our praying should build on the Lord's Prayer. How we enlarge on each petition, filling out each one in a way that faithfully reflects what Jesus meant, becomes a superstructure on that foundation.

The Lord's Prayer therefore is the foundation; our own praying is the superstructure. The foundation is not intended to be the way we are to pray verbatim all the time. I repeat: it is certainly good to pray the Lord's Prayer, even daily, privately or publicly. But it is not the way we should always pray or what we should recite every time we turn to God.

New Testament scholar Don Carson noted how ironic it is that the context of the Lord's Prayer in the Sermon on the Mount forbids meaningless repetition in prayer, and yet no prayer has been repeated more than this, too often without understanding. Even the *Didache* (known as the "teaching of the Twelve," from the second century) prescribes that Christians should repeat this prayer three times a day. This is surely unnecessary. There are several prayers in the New Testament and in the Book of Acts. The Lord's Prayer is not mentioned. Jesus did not say that this is the only way to pray. He Himself prayed several other times, and it was not this prayer.

There are, of course, many times a day we will turn to God without remembering the order of the Lord's Prayer. In a perfect world we keep our Lord's order in mind: who God is, where He is, what His interests are, and so forth. But there are times when in desperation we simply cry out: "God!" "Jesus!" "Lord, help me!" And He hears us. So do not take this book to imply that all praying must be a literal filling out of the order and content of the Lord's Prayer.

Jesus is *teaching* us how to pray. He sets before us the model prayer, the perfect prayer. We should learn from it and hopefully make it the way we pray when we seek God's face. And we should do so as much as possible.

How you and I pray, then, should as much as possible be an extension or filling out of the Lord's Prayer; it should be a superstructure on top of the foundation that builds on what Jesus gave us. All good praying will be consistent with the original words of the Lord's Prayer. Throughout church history people have marveled at this prayer. Men such as St. Augustine and Martin Luther have observed that there is nothing more wonderful in the entire Bible than the

Lord's Prayer. John Calvin stated that the petitions include everything that we may rightly wish from God.

Do not forget that it is a commanded prayer. When you pray, Jesus said, "Say" (Luke 11:2). This is stated in the imperative mood; it is how we should pray. "This, then, is how you should pray" (Matt. 6:9). It is also a corporate prayer. "You" is second person plural in the Greek. Not only that, but when Jesus says to pray, "Our Father," it reflects all of God's people, not one person, praying. It is the church's prayer—how "you" should pray—not how Jesus prays. After all, He did not need to pray for forgiveness. It is a perfectly worded and correct prayer; we are told exactly what to say. It is a complete prayer. There are six petitions (some would say seven, depending on how you count "And lead us not into temptation, but deliver us from the evil one"), which include everything we may rightly wish from God. As the Law was in two tables—the first part with reference to God, the second to humankind—so the first three petitions here focus on God's glory, the second part on our benefits.

Interpreting the Will of God

Since to pray the Lord's Prayer is to be sure you are praying perfectly in the will of God, so too may we be confident we are praying in the will of God as long as what we utter reflects this prayer faithfully. If we can remember that the unembellished Lord's Prayer is the foundation, our own praying being the superstructure, we can have confidence that our praying is in the will of God.

In 1 Corinthians 3 Paul talks about a superstructure being comprised of gold, silver, and precious stones, but also wood, hay, and straw, referring to our lives in anticipation of the judgment seat of Christ (1 Cor. 3:12–15). The point here is that the superstructure that will stand the test at the final judgment is one comprised of gold, silver, and precious stones. Such will not burn up when the fire is revealed. The wood, hay, and straw will be consumed.

I would borrow this analogy and apply it to our praying. I would therefore urge that we pray in a manner that demonstrates gold, silver, and precious stones. This would be praying in the will of God; it would reflect the beauty and honor of God. Asking amiss—praying wrongly and contrary to the will of God—would be using wood, hay, and straw in erecting a superstructure that will not stand the test.

The purpose of this book is not only to examine each line of the Lord's Prayer but to learn how to interpret the will of God. If you understand the Lord's Prayer, you will be more able to pray in His will. You will develop a spiritual aptitude that equips you to pray rightly and not wrongly. You will develop a spiritual sense that sets off an inner warning, "Do not go here," when you begin to ask amiss. This comes by knowing what each petition means. As long as your praying is a faithful and true extension of each of the petitions, you will sense a Voice that says, "This is the way; walk in it" (Isa. 30:21). I am not saying you will always know that what you ask for is what God wants for you. Even Paul admitted he did not always know how to pray (Rom. 8:26–27). But it does mean that you will be spared of continually asking for what is displeasing to God.

As we will see later in this book, if we can develop a sensitivity to the Holy Spirit it will greatly enable us to pray in the will of God. As you know, the context of the Lord's Prayer in Matthew is the Sermon on the Mount, and the focus of that sermon is the kingdom of heaven. The kingdom of heaven is best defined as *the conscious presence and enabling grace of God*. When you learn to recognize the conscious presence of God, which comes partly from developing a sensitivity to the Holy Spirit, you will find yourself praying more and more in the will of God and in sync with the Lord's Prayer. This is because when you begin to wander outside what God wants, you will sense a lack of peace and a lack of the consciousness of God's presence. That is a warning to *stop*, to not pray in that direction any longer. It comes because you have developed an intimacy with the Holy Spirit. This issue will come up again in this book.

The way to know you are praying in the will of God, then, is to keep the Lord's Prayer in mind. Remember the pattern, the content and purpose of it. This book is designed not only to give an exposition of the Lord's Prayer but also to help you know if you are praying in the will of God. It is not a book that will enable a person to twist God's arm. You cannot make the God of the Bible do what *you* want. But if you delight yourself in the Lord, He will give you the desires of your heart (Ps. 37:4). That is His promise; it is a guarantee.

If you can find yourself delighting in the Lord's Prayer, then it is a good sign—a very good sign—that you are delighting in God Himself. This means that the desires of your heart will be yours, sooner or later. The test, however, is whether you will affirm the foundation—the Lord's Prayer itself—and build on it with materials that magnificently show you want to pray in God's will. If you do, congratulations! This means you are pleasing the Lord and your praying is being *heard* in heaven.

CHAPTER 2

THE FATHERHOOD OF GOD

Our Father...
—MATTHEW 6:9

IN HIS INVOCATION at the inauguration of President Barack Obama, Pastor Rick Warren closed his prayer with the Lord's Prayer. Although he referred to the Jewish *Shema* ("Hear, O Israel: The LORD our God, the LORD is one") and endeavored to show appropriate respect to all cultural backgrounds, Warren received criticism from some people who felt that the Lord's Prayer made the occasion completely "Christian." And yet there have been *Christians* who criticized the Lord's Prayer generally on the basis that it is *not* a Christian prayer! Some have opined that since the prayer does not end in the words "in Jesus' name," it is not a prayer Christians should pray.

However, Rick Warren did something very intriguing and bold. He ended his own prayer by introducing the Lord's Prayer in a manner that left no doubt his inaugural prayer would be prayed explicitly in Jesus' name. Having prayed that President Obama and his family would be committed to God's loving care, Pastor Warren concluded: "I humbly ask this in the name of the One who changed my life: *Yeshua* [Hebrew for Jesus], *Essa* [Arabic for Jesus], *Jesus* [Spanish for Jesus], Jesus [English], who taught us to pray: 'Our Father who art in heaven.'"

What if Pastor Warren had merely ended his inaugural prayer with the Lord's Prayer? Would it have been a Christian prayer? Yes. This is because praying in Christ's name is implicit, said Dr. Martyn Lloyd-Jones. "No man can truly say 'Our Father which art in heaven,' save one who knows the Lord Jesus Christ and who is in Christ."[1] He went on to say, "It is only those who are true believers in the Lord Jesus Christ who can say, 'Our Father.'"[2] In other words, only the Christian—and the Lord Jesus Himself—has the right to call God *Father*.

Why is this? First, the Lord's Prayer was given to *believers*—Jesus' disciples—who are told to pray this prayer. Whether you take it from the Sermon on the Mount (Matt. 6:9–13) or Luke's account, which shows Jesus responding to their request, "Lord, teach us to pray" (Luke 11:1–4), the prayer was designed for believers. The assumption in the Sermon on the Mount is that His followers have taken on board what Jesus stated in this discourse up to that point—for example, the Beatitudes (Matt. 5:3–12), His teaching about the Law and His promise to fulfill it (vv. 17–20), the way He applied the Law (vv. 21–42), His teaching on blessing your enemies (vv. 43–48), and what He said about praying not to be seen of men (6:1–8). He would not have brought in the Lord's Prayer to those who did not believe what He had taught already.

Second, it can never be stressed too often that Jesus is the eternal Son of God, the Father's one and only Son. Jesus has a unique relationship with the Father. We are children of

God, yes, but this relationship is made possible only through Jesus. He came unto His own (the Jews), but "his own did not receive him. Yet to *all who received him, to those who believed in his name*, he gave the right to become *children of God*—children born not of natural descent, nor of human decision or a husband's will, but born of God" (John 1:11–13, emphasis mine). In a word: only those who receive Him and believe in His name have the right to be children of God and therefore to pray the Lord's Prayer.

Nobody Needs to Feel Left Out

If you feel left out because you are not a believer, would *you* like to have the right to pray the Lord's Prayer? This right is offered to you—right now. You don't need to feel deprived, rejected, or left out. All you have to do is receive Jesus— right now. He is being offered to you—right now.

First recognize that you need a Savior. You cannot save yourself. If you could, there would have been no need for God to send His Son into the world. The angel said to the shepherds, "Today in the town of David a Savior has been born to you; he is Christ the Lord" (Luke 2:11). A major part of His being Savior is that Jesus never sinned—ever. He fulfilled the holy, perfect Law of Moses (Matt. 5:17). Therefore when He died on the cross at the age of thirty-three, He said, "It is finished" (John 19:30). In these words He acknowledged that He had kept the Law and fulfilled His mission on earth. Not only that, the words "It is finished" are a translation of the Greek word *tetelestai*, which was a colloquial expression in the ancient marketplace that meant "paid in full."[3] Jesus paid the entire debt you owe to God by dying for you. *If you can accept this*, which is what is meant by "receiving Jesus and believing in His name," you qualify to pray the Lord's Prayer. But I would suggest nonetheless, so your relationship with God is clear in your mind, that you pray the following right now:

> Lord Jesus Christ, I need You. I want You. I am sorry for my sins. I know I cannot save myself. Thank You for dying on the cross for my sins. Wash my sins away by Your blood. I welcome Your Holy Spirit into my heart. As best I know how, I give You my life. Amen.

Now you are qualified to pray the Lord's Prayer.

Congratulations! Welcome to the family of God. You have just become a member. You have been born again. You are now a Christian. There are various other words for what has just happened to you, such as *converted, saved, regenerated, justified*.

However, there could be an exception to what I have been saying. It is possible that a person can actually become a Christian by praying the Lord's Prayer—if they understand what they are saying and mean what they are saying. In other words, praying the Lord's Prayer could be the very way a person is brought into a true relationship with God.

This is why it is a good thing for the Lord's Prayer to be prayed publicly, with unbelievers present. The Lord's Prayer *could* become an evangelistic tool. God can use the Lord's Prayer to awaken a person's soul and bring them to Himself, even if it does not happen the first time they pray it. Would you be surprised if someone was actually converted when Pastor Rick Warren led countless millions to pray the Lord's Prayer, especially if they had heard the prayer before?

We must not forget that although it can be prayed by individual believers, the Lord's Prayer is a corporate prayer. You know that Jesus told the disciples to pray this. "When you [second person plural in the Greek] pray," He said to them. Therefore, it follows that we pray, "*Our* Father," not "my Father." That is humbling, and it puts all of us in equal standing before God. No person can claim to be God's "favorite" or to be special. No one can claim to be more accepted by God because he or she has been a Christian for a longer period of time, or because he or she has done some pious duty more than others. Neither should anyone think they are at the "head of the queue" because they have suffered a lot, have a handicap, have been neglected, or have been mistreated. God is my Father, yes; but He is your Father too. And when we address Him as we are told to do in the Lord's Prayer, we simultaneously affirm our standing both with God and the rest of the body of Christ as well.

When we pray the Lord's Prayer, then, we join a multitude "no one could count, from every nation, tribe, people and language" (Rev. 7:9). Each of us is one out of many. I pray the Lord's Prayer and get the Father's full attention while knowing full well that He equally and simultaneously listens to others—tens of millions and millions all at once, with equal concern for each of them. One aspect of prayer that makes it miraculous is that God not only loves every person as if there were no one else to love, as St. Augustine put it, but *listens* to every person as if there were no one else praying. I must not forget that when I address God as Jesus has taught us, I pray, "*Our* Father."

There Are Other Names by
Which We Address God

Jesus is not trying to tell us that addressing God as "Father" is the only way to call on Him. There are other prayers in the New Testament that do not address Him as Father. The first recorded prayer after Jesus ascended to heaven shows the disciples addressing God as *Lord*: "Lord, you know everyone's heart. Show us which of these two you have chosen to take over this apostolic ministry" (Acts 1:24–25).

The next corporate prayer by the church that is recorded shows they "raised their voices together in prayer to God," saying: "Sovereign Lord…you made the heaven and the earth and the sea, and everything in them" (Acts 4:24). They may have assumed God the Father when they said "Sovereign Lord," but they could have meant Jesus. This shows that we are not required necessarily to address God as Father each time we pray. Stephen prayed just before he went to heaven, "Lord Jesus, receive my spirit" (Acts 7:59). On the Damascus Road, Saul—the future apostle Paul—certainly meant Jesus when he said, "Who are you, Lord?" (Acts 9:5). Peter was apparently talking to Jesus when he said, "Surely not, Lord!" (Acts 10:14).

This brings up another interesting question: Can we pray directly to the Holy Spirit? Yes. *Because He is God.* The three persons of the Trinity are equally divine: God the Father, God the Son, and God the Holy Spirit. Although there are no recorded prayers in the Bible showing that someone addressed the Holy Spirit directly, there are countless examples in our hymnody: "Come, Holy Ghost, all-quickening fire" (Charles Wesley); "Holy Spirit, truth divine, dawn upon this soul of mine" (Samuel Longfellow); "Lord God the Holy Ghost, in this accepted hour, as on the day of Pentecost, descend in all Thy power" (James Montgomery); "Spirit of God, descend upon my heart" (George Croly); "Breathe on me, Breath of God" (Edwin Hatch); and many more. If it is appropriate to *sing* to the Holy Spirit, it is surely right to pray to Him.

My point is this: although the Lord's Prayer is a pattern prayer, it is not meant to be the only way we pray but rather to be seen as a skeleton that we have to clothe. The apostle Paul offered many prayers in behalf of Christians and repeatedly showed that he prayed to the Father (see Eph. 1:17, 3:14, 5:20; Col. 1:3, 12, 3:17; 1 Thess. 1:3, 3:11).

The Term "Fatherhood of God" Can Be Abused

The phrase "Fatherhood of God" is a lovely phrase, but it has been taken over by many unbelieving people who deny that Jesus is the only way to God and the only way to heaven. Some would add to these words and say they believe in the Fatherhood of God and the brotherhood of man. The idea is expressed by these people that God is the Father of everybody, saved or lost. They would add that everyone is our brother or sister, whether or not they are believers. Some would say that people don't need to be converted in the first place to have God as their Father, that He already is the Father of all. They would say it is not necessary to pray in the name of Jesus, because all people are equally God's children whether they come to faith in Christ or not. This teaching is alien to the New Testament and an utter denial of the true Christian faith.

And yet the term "Fatherhood of God" is a good and proper phrase, rightly understood. Therefore, the Fatherhood of God needs to be defined and explained. So too the phrase "brotherhood of man," a good term, rightly understood.

John Stott observed that the essential difference between pharisaical, pagan, and Christian praying lies in the kind of God we pray to. In telling us to address God as "Our Father in heaven," Jesus' concern is not with protocol but with the consciousness that we might come to God in the right frame of mind. We need to know at least some elementary truths about the God of the Bible. It is a wonderful privilege to talk to Him. But the very reason for this skeleton prayer is that we might know something of the true God. It is always wise, before we pray, to meditate by recalling who He is.

The idea of God being our Father is almost entirely a New Testament teaching. The term *father* with respect to God does occur in the Old Testament, but not with reference to addressing God. He is called "a father to the fatherless, a defender of widows, is God in his holy dwelling" (Ps. 68:5). "As a father has compassion on his children, so the LORD has compassion on those who fear him" (Ps. 103:13). Isaiah comes close to addressing God as Father, but not quite: "But you are our Father, though Abraham does not know us... you, O LORD, are our Father, our Redeemer from of old is your name" (Isa. 63:16). "Yet, O LORD, you are our Father. We are the clay, you are the potter; we are all the work of your hand" (Isa. 64:8).

It was Jesus who explicitly addressed God as Father. He was the unique Son of God. He was and is God's only "natural" Son. God is uniquely His Father. We are made children of God by adoption. We have been adopted into the same family (Rom. 8:15; Eph. 1:5). Not only does Jesus address God as Father, He also commands us to address God in the same way. There is no sibling rivalry, no jealousy whatever, between Jesus and the children of God. Let me share one of the most dazzling truths I know: God loves you as much as He loves Jesus! That's right—we are joint heirs, co-heirs, with Jesus. Jesus even prayed that the world would see that the Father loved His family "even as you have loved me" (John 17:23).

There are many people, perhaps some who read these lines, who know what it is to have both an adopted child as well as a natural offspring. They love both equally. They will tell you that they can *tell no difference* in the love they feel for each. I have talked with a number of parents who testify to this. That is the way the Father is with Jesus and that countless multitude! He loves us as much as He loves His own Son. Not only that, but we are as secure in the family of God as Jesus Himself is in the Godhead. What do you suppose the chances are that Jesus could be dislodged, or disenfranchised, from the Trinity? None—absolutely none. So are we kept secure, eternally secure, in the family of God. We are loved with an "everlasting love" (Jer. 31:3). "Both the one who makes men holy and those who are made holy are of the same family. So Jesus is not ashamed to call them brothers" (Heb. 2:11).

It is true that all men and all women everywhere are God's children in a sense—and each of them are brothers and sisters in a sense. This is because we have been created in the image of God (Gen. 1:27). Human beings all have in common that they are made in God's image, unlike plant life or animals. When Paul addressed the philosophers of Athens at the Areopagus, he quoted one of the Greek poets—"We are his offspring"—showing that all of us are God's offspring (Acts 17:28–29). God made every single human being who ever lived, and He is upholding each of them as Creator and sustainer.

But this is not the same thing as being God's adopted children. The Bible makes a sharp distinction between those who belong to God and those who do not. This is the major point John wanted to make: "See what great love the Father has lavished on us, that we should be called children of God!" (1 John 3:1). He immediately contrasts this with the world: "The reason the world does not know us is that it did not know him" (1 John 3:1). Jesus clearly said in His high priestly prayer, "I am not praying for the world, but for those you have given me, for they are yours" (John 17:9). This is an unmistakable contrast between those who are God's children and those who are not. Jesus even said of certain Jews, "You belong to your father, the devil" (John 8:44). In a word: the Fatherhood of God is a good and valid term, but only when it refers to the fact of our being adopted into the family by God's grace. And when Jesus told us to address God as Father, He was speaking to believers.

Understanding God as Father

How do we understand God as Father? He is personal. Theologian Paul Tillich wanted to define God as the ground of all being, which is panentheism. This is simply not compatible with the notion of God's divine Fatherhood. God is just as personal as we are, only more so. Theologian Joachim Jeremias has shown how exceptional and stunning Jesus' use of addressing God as Father must have been at first to His Jewish disciples. Jews in ancient times preferred only exalted titles for God. They would address him as Sovereign Lord or King of the Universe. Jesus even used the Aramaic *abba*, the word used by children to address their father, "daddy." Our adoption into the family makes us joint heirs with Jesus; hence, "we cry, '*Abba*, Father'" (Rom. 8:15).

He is the perfect Father, a being "than whom no greater can be conceived," as Anselm (c. 1033–1109), archbishop of Canterbury, put it. For those who have not had a good relationship with their parent, there is difficulty in calling him "Father." I can sympathize with this. I love and honor my dad and feel I was exceptionally blessed to have the parents I had. But I always felt I did not come up to my father's standard. A's and B's weren't good enough on my report card; my dad wanted all A's—and no A-minuses! And yet this is to say nothing of those who grew up being abused. People like this have extreme difficulty—some never get over it—calling God "Father."

If you have trouble calling God "Father," try to remember that Jesus said, "Anyone who has seen me has seen the Father" (John 14:9). Get your image of God from Jesus, not from your earthly parent. Picture Jesus, of whom it was absolutely true, "A bruised reed he will not break" (Matt. 12:20). Picture Jesus, who could not bear to see somebody deeply hurt. "Don't cry," He pleaded with the widow who was burying her only son (Luke 7:13). Picture Jesus, who is able to sympathize with all of us to the hilt (Heb. 4:15). Picture Jesus, who accepts us as we are, who never moralizes and never shames us when we slip and fall. He is the perfect Father. When our parents disciplined us, said the writer to the Hebrews, they did so "as they thought best." So often that is not good enough. But when the perfect Father disciplines us, He never loses His temper or punishes us to impress anybody; He does what is absolutely for our good (Heb. 12:10).

Remember this: when God chastens us—and we all need it from time to time—He does not do it to "get even." He does not play "tit for tat." God got even at the cross! "As far as the east is from the west, so far has he removed our transgressions from us" (Ps. 103:12). God never disciplines us to prove anything. The greatest freedom is having nothing to prove, and God has nothing to prove. He disciplines us for one reason: He loves us (Heb. 12:6). He wants us to be partakers of His holiness (Heb. 12:11).

Our heavenly Father is, furthermore, *always present*. "God is our refuge and strength, an ever-present help in trouble" (Ps. 46:1). "Where can I go from your Spirit? Where can I flee from your presence? If I go up to the heavens, you are there; if I make my bed in the depths, you are there. If I rise on the wings of the dawn, if I settle on the far side of the sea, even there your hand will guide me, your right hand will hold me fast" (Ps. 139:7–10). The best of parents cannot always be present. It may be that they are busy, preoccupied, or have to be elsewhere. They cannot be in two places at once. But God is always present with us. As He listens to each of us as though no one else were addressing Him, so also He is with each of us as though He were nowhere else.

Some grow up with an absentee parent, especially a father who is never around. I fear that I myself have been this way with our children more than I care to admit. In *Totally Forgiving Ourselves*, I lament that I put my church first, thinking I was putting God first, as our precious son and daughter grew up in London. I now believe that if I had put my family first I would have preached just as well, but I cannot get those years back. I have had to forgive myself, which I have done. But it cannot erase the deprivation that our children did not deserve. In any case, God is the perfect Father—always there, always present, always available, always listening. He is in heaven, yes; but He is equally here with us. He is closer than our hands or feet, closer than the air we breathe. He is but a cry away. We don't have to remember the skeleton outline of the Lord's Prayer. As I have said, we can just cry "God!" or "Jesus!" and He is there.

The Fatherhood of God implies the existence of a family, especially when we realize the implications of saying "our" Father. In his prayer for the Ephesians, Paul said he knelt before the Father, "from whom every family in heaven and on earth derives its name" (Eph. 3:15). It is another reminder that I am *one out of many* (Rev. 7:9). The multitude that no one is able to count is made up of those God predestined to be the "firstborn among many brothers and sisters" (Rom. 8:29).

The Fatherhood of God points to equity in the family. Said Peter, "You call on a Father who judges each person's work impartially" (1 Pet. 1:17). God treats every member of the family with absolute equity. He is another person's Father as well as yours. It is a sober reminder that should your enemy be a Christian, the Father loves that brother or sister as much as He does you. Our Father does not want quarreling in the family. How do you feel when your children quarrel? This is partly why we have the petition, which I will deal with in considerable detail in a subsequent chapter, "Forgive us our trespasses, as we forgive those who trespass against us."

I must come back to the point this chapter began with: this teaching also indicates the exclusiveness of God's family. I'm sorry, but God is not the Father of all people indiscriminately. Although Jesus died for all people indiscriminately (John 3:16, Heb. 2:9), not all for whom Christ died *receive*

Him as their Savior. You may be interested to know that the early church prohibited non-Christians from reciting this prayer as vigorously as they forbade them from joining with believers at the Lord's table. While I myself think they may have gone too far by keeping certain people from praying this prayer, this practice does indicate that the Lord's Prayer implies the exclusiveness of God's family.

The only time Jesus addressed the Father as "God"—not as "Father"—was when He cried out on the cross, "My God, my God, why have you forsaken me?" (Matt. 27:46). That was the precise moment the righteous Son who knew no sin was made sin for us (2 Cor. 5:21). This was the moment Isaiah saw hundreds of years in advance when "the LORD has laid on him the iniquity of us all" (Isa. 53:6).

It is a reminder that when we say "Our Father," we approach a Father whose justice has been satisfied, once for all. He therefore has no swings of mood; He holds no grudges. He is never diverted from listening to us because He is preoccupied with someone else's problem or a problem of His own. He is happy with Himself and is content to listen to each of us. He knows how we are formed, remembers that we are dust (Ps. 103:14). The perfect Father calls us to pray—and He gives us the perfect prayer. It leaves nothing out that we need.

CHAPTER 3

BEING PUT IN OUR PLACE

...in heaven.
—MATTHEW 6:9

D O YOU KNOW what it is like to be put in your place? As I was preparing this chapter, for some reason an embarrassing memory came into my mind which I thought I would share. It goes back to 1953, when I was an eighteen-year-old freshman at Trevecca Nazarene College (now Trevecca Nazarene University). I had enrolled in a New Testament course. Claude Galloway was the professor. We went through the New Testament that semester from Matthew to Revelation. On the week before we got to the Book of Revelation, Professor Galloway said, "Next week we come to the Book of Revelation. Frankly, I am not sure I understand this book. Does anybody here understand it?"

My immodest hand went up. "Oh, Brother Kendall, would you like to teach the course next week?"

"I certainly will," I replied with absolutely no shame. The day came. I had looked forward to what I imagined as my finest hour. I expected the anointing to come down on these poor, ignorant students and the deprived professor with such power that all would need to be carried to their next classes.

I taught the Book of Revelation that day (as I understood it then). I thought I was at my best. Nothing was so clear to me. I spoke with stunning authority. On a scale of one to ten regarding confidence, I was a twelve. But when my lecture was over, it was over. The members of the class, about thirty, filed out quietly. Not a soul spoke to me except one student, who said, "Do you always let your lower jaw fall to one side like that when you speak?" Then he left. Only the professor hung around. I expected his accolades. He simply said, "Well, Brother Kendall, you may be right. That is the view I used to take, but I'm not so sure now. Thanks for doing this. Nice try."

I was devastated. Humiliated. I got what I deserved. I was put in my place.

The words "in heaven" are meant to put us in our place—but without the kind of embarrassment I just described. That our Father is "in heaven" should give us a feeling of awe, true reverence, an awareness that we are but one among many, and keep us from rushing thoughtlessly into God's presence. If we understand why Jesus put these words there, it will help us to know Him better. It will help us know ourselves better. Merely repeating these words may not reveal why they are there. I am sure you could pray the Lord's Prayer many times without grasping the reason for these carefully chosen words.

If you are used to praying "Our Father which art in heaven," keep in mind that is the King James Version, which most of us are used to using when we say the Lord's Prayer. I happen to love it—and I still pray this as in the KJV. However, for this book I am mostly using the New International Version, which uses modern language.

So have you ever wondered what the Lord's Prayer would be like had Jesus not added these words, "in heaven"? Did you think this was an incidental, if not redundant, phrase simply to explain that the Father dwells in heaven? Jesus is doing far more than merely telling us where God the Father lives. The two words "in heaven" are at the beginning of the Lord's Prayer to help us see our place—to humble us—and give us some objectivity about ourselves. It is not that God rebukes us or slaps us on the wrist by these two words. It is rather that our Lord intended to give us a perspective that should help us see our place before the Father.

Has it occurred to you that your Father in heaven—along with Jesus at His right hand—is already being worshipped there, whether or not we pray to Him? There are billions and billions of angels that praise and worship Him sixty seconds a minute, sixty minutes an hour, twenty-four hours a day, seven days a week, every day of the year. The seraphs worship, saying, "Holy, holy, holy is the LORD Almighty; the whole earth is full of his glory" (Isa. 6:3). The four living creatures never stop praising God day and night: "Holy, holy, holy is the Lord God Almighty, who was, and is, and is to come" (Rev. 4:8). All of those now with the Lord—Abraham, Isaac, Jacob, Isaiah, Daniel, the apostles, our departed loved ones who are in Christ—are worshipping Him day and night.

We also are to worship God day and night here on earth. But it is not physically possible for us to do this as we will in heaven. We can, however, continually offer to God our spiritual worship, as Paul puts it in Romans 12:1. So much worship here below is vain worship, as Jesus said to the

Pharisees (Mark 7:6–7). When we get to heaven we will worship without any constraints because we will have glorified bodies without sin (Rom. 8:30).

You may ask, "Does God really need our worship? What can you and I add to Him by praying the Lord's Prayer?"

This is what is so amazing. He still wants you and me to talk to Him. He wants our attention. He likes our company. He listens to each of us as if there were no one else, though He is hearing countless cries and praises to Him all the time. Jesus simply wants us to be aware of this when we talk to God. He is in heaven where He is extolled, adored, and honored continually by praise and worship.

Two Old Testament passages are relevant here:

> Guard your steps when you go to the house of God. Go near to listen rather than to offer the sacrifice of fools, who do not know that they do wrong. Do not be quick with your mouth, do not be hasty in your heart to utter anything before God. God is in heaven and you are on earth, so let your words be few. As a dream comes when there are many cares, so the speech of a fool when there are many words.
> —ECCLESIASTES 5:1–3

> Our God is in heaven; he does whatever pleases him.
> —PSALM 115:3

God is in heaven, and we are on earth. That is a simple but very profound fact.

Taking Ourselves Too Seriously

To put it another way, the purpose of the phrase "Father in heaven" is to keep us from taking ourselves too seriously—and our heavenly Father not seriously enough. Jesus is the first ever to pray to the Father, that is, to call Him "Father" and to teach us to call Him that. As we saw earlier, Jesus also would refer to *Abba* Father, Aramaic for our equivalent of "Daddy." And we are not discouraged from feeling or doing the same. Far from it! Being adopted into the family of God, we are loved with the same love that the Father has for Jesus, and we also have the same security He has. That security and intimacy are part of our being in the family.

However, by adding these words "in heaven" Jesus reminds us how big and how great God is. This is partly to ensure also that we will never become overly familiar with Him.

A few years ago, someone who was said to have a prophetic gift had a "word" for me, namely, that I should start calling God "Daddy" in my private quiet time. Since Paul admonished us not to despise prophesying, to prove all things, and to hold on to the good (1 Thess. 5:20–21), I tried it for a while. I would not want to criticize you if you do this—or if you call God "Papa," as a friend of mine does. But for me it was contrived and unnatural. Not everyone needs to use the word *Daddy* in addressing God to experience intimacy. But there is nothing wrong with this, and I am sure God Himself does not mind.

In this chapter, we are to see that "Our Father in heaven" encompasses two perspectives in approaching God. "Our Father" invites intimacy with God; "in heaven" points to His supreme majesty. Therefore, "Our Father in heaven" simultaneously embraces both approaches to God. And although they may seem contradictory, we are to approach God with a feeling of awe and intimacy at the same time.

Implied in this discussion is a conviction I have taught all over the world—namely, that there has been a silent divorce in the church, speaking generally, between the Word and the Spirit. When there is a divorce, sometimes the children stay with the mother, sometimes with the father. In this divorce you have those on the "Word" side and those on the "Spirit" side. Those on the Word side stress God's sovereignty and majesty—the need to uphold the faith once delivered to the saints, a return to the God of Martin Luther and Jonathan Edwards, an emphasis upon expository preaching. These people also tend to sing the old hymns, especially such as those of Isaac Watts and Charles Wesley. Those on the Spirit side emphasize signs, wonders, and miracles—spiritual power as we see in the Book of Acts, where prayer meetings resulted in small earthquakes; where getting in Peter's shadow meant supernatural healing; where lying to the Holy Spirit brought instant death. These people also tend to sing new songs and choruses.

It is my view that *both* sides are essentially right and that one emphasis without the other creates an imbalance, plus a very inadequate presentation of the gospel. It will not result in a restoration of the honor of God's name so desperately needed at the present time.

Consider for a moment how some "Word" people may at times address God—and do so in a hushed, holy, and respectful tone: "Almighty and most holy God, our sovereign Savior and gracious Lord, we come humbly into Your presence." For people who are introduced to the Christian faith in this kind of atmosphere, two reactions sometimes follow: (1) a feeling that this is the only way to approach the true God and (2) a feeling that this God is remote and unknowable. Those who have the latter reaction are often ready to listen to an approach to God that does not make Him appear so remote, if not harsh.

God is Spirit (John 4:24). That is why faith is required. What makes faith *faith* is that we cannot see God with our natural eye. "No one has ever seen God, but the one and only Son, who is himself God and is in closest relationship with the Father, has made him known" (John 1:18). "Though you have not seen him, you love him; and even though you do not see him now, you believe in him and are filled with an inexpressible and glorious joy" (1 Pet. 1:8). One of the chief reasons for the second commandment ("You shall not make for yourself an image in the form of anything in heaven above or on the earth beneath or in the waters below," Exod. 20:4) is to make room for faith. An idol is visible and requires no faith to see it; it plays into our fleshly nature to want to see before we believe. Faith, however, "is confidence in what we hope for and assurance about what *we do not see*" (Heb. 11:1, emphasis mine). When you see the person you are talking to, you don't need to exercise faith that you are talking to them. You do, however, with your heavenly Father.

God's Independence

Jesus even wants to show the Father's independence. God is in heaven, and when He is as high as the heavens are above the earth, you know you can't snap your fingers and expect service. When I was in Kenya I saw an aristocratic man snap his fingers at a servant—and that servant came running in a split second. I was startled to watch this. I didn't think this sort of thing went on nowadays. And yet there are those who have an attitude toward God that they can snap their fingers and expect God to jump! In reality it should be the other way around: if God were to snap His fingers, *we* are the ones to jump. This was the main point of one of the psalms of ascent: "As the eyes of slaves look to the hand of their master, as the eyes of a female slave look to the hand of her mistress, so our eyes look to the LORD our God, till he shows us his mercy" (Ps. 123:2). The picture is that of a slave whose eyes are so focused on their master's hands that they are ready to obey in a split second. Therefore we should look to God and want to be ready when He calls for us. We are fortunate whenever He beckons for our attention. The truth is, God can give or withhold mercy and still be just. He does not need us; He is not tied to us; He is not dependent on us.

However, it is extraordinary to think that God confides in us (Ps. 25:14). He called Abraham His friend (Isa. 41:8; Jas. 2:23). Abraham is a type of the Christian believer (Gen. 15:6; Rom. 4:1–5). We should follow Abraham in our faith and also in seeking to be God's friend.

God's independence is a missing note in much Christian thinking today. We all need to see that God is not controlled by us and that He certainly doesn't want us to try to control Him. He does not need our wisdom. He does not consult the highest archangel, or any of us, to know what to do next. "The God who made the world and everything in it is the Lord of heaven and earth and does not live in temples built by human hands. And he is not served by human hands, as if he needed anything. Rather, he himself gives everyone life and breath and everything else" (Acts 17:24–25). Our Father in heaven is not dependent upon His creation but remains independent. He has not turned over the reins to His mortal, finite creatures. When we therefore pray, "Our Father in heaven," we affirm two things: (1) His independence and (2) our dependence and need of Him.

God's Inscrutability

There is more: "Our Father in heaven" refers to God's inscrutability. This means He is impossible to understand except in measure. This means you can never fully, ultimately figure Him out. If you think you know Him and know what He is up to, you will probably realize very soon how little you knew! You think you understand Him, then shortly you realize you have hardly begun to understand Him. "My thoughts are not your thoughts....As the heavens are higher than the earth, so are my ways higher than your ways and my thoughts than your thoughts" (Isa. 55:8–9). And again: "Our God is in heaven; he does whatever pleases him" (Ps. 115:3).

You cannot predict what He will do; you cannot even completely fathom what He has done already. "Oh, the depth of the riches of the wisdom and knowledge of God! How unsearchable his judgments, and his paths beyond tracing out! Who has known the mind of the Lord? Or who has been his counselor? Who has ever given to God, that God should repay them? For from him and through him and for him are all things. To him be the glory forever! Amen" (Rom. 11:33–36). God is in heaven; you are on earth. He is in control; you are not in control of Him.

Be careful if you say that you know for sure what God is going to do. As Rob Parsons sometimes says, "If you want to make God smile, tell him your plans." When Moses saw the burning bush that was not consumed, he reckoned he would get to the bottom of it. God said, *Stop!* "Do not come any closer....Take off your sandals, for the place where you are standing is holy ground" (Exod. 3:5). Moses was not allowed to figure out what was going on. Nobody knew why Jesus of

Nazareth was dying on a cross until after it happened and the Holy Spirit came to explain. And all of us are still trying to take this in. God is in heaven and is inscrutable. Don't try to figure Him out.

Being Overly Familiar With God

Is being overly familiar with God a bad thing? Yes. Why is it wrong, and what is the consequence of an overfamiliarity with God? Familiarity means assuming a greater degree of informality or friendship than is proper. It is when you know a person almost too well and begin to presume. It is when you cross over from respect and awesome reverence to impertinence. It is when you begin to control a relationship and forget another's personhood. When that happens in a human relationship, something is lost; one feels used. Any lasting relationship is based upon mutual respect, when neither person becomes manipulative, manipulated, or used.

Overfamiliarity sometimes happens in one's relationship with God. It is when you think you know God so well. It is when you begin to think you have a claim on God—that He is indebted to you, that He owes you something. It is also when you think you have fully understood Him and are closer to Him than anybody else is. You feel too special. You feel He needs you. You feel He has told you so much that you have a relationship with Him like no one else has.

This kind of thing can begin innocently; no harm by us is intended. For example, it may begin when God draws very near to you; you feel His presence, His power. You feel a definite sense of guidance. You are able to pray with liberty. But before you know it, you imagine He has communicated more than He Himself actually told you! You begin to presume; you think you know so much. It is not unlike when Joseph and Mary thought Jesus was in their company and proceeded without Him (Luke 2:43–44). I have done this more times than I would want you to know.

What happens then? Usually a huge disappointment. God may hide His face and withdraw Himself, and you feel suddenly alone and betrayed. You wonder if you really knew God at all. You feel angry. Joseph and Mary actually felt angry with Jesus: "Why have you treated us like this?" Mary said to Him (Luke 2:48).

When God Hides His Face

What, then, is truly going on? The answer is: God hides Himself for our good. This hiding is like a cleansing process; it rids us of thoughts we put there and that God didn't put there at all.

Nobody took himself more seriously than Elijah. He regarded himself as the only prophet on earth. "I am the only one of the LORD's prophets left" (1 Kings 18:22). Not only was Elijah completely wrong to say this; the boldness he exhibited on Mount Carmel (1 Kings 18:24–40) was followed by his being scared to death the next day, when Jezebel was trying to find him (1 Kings 19:1–3). Elijah was gently and lovingly put in his place (1 Kings 19:15–18). The psalmist, in a depressed frame of mind, said, "Darkness is my closest friend" (Ps. 88:18). At such times God seems to betray us, having previously been so real to us.

It is not that God really does betray us; He only seems to do so. It is sometimes His way of saving us from ourselves. He must be true to Himself. After all, the buck stops with

Him. He does us no favor to let us manipulate Him, to let us think we know Him better than we actually do, or to let us see Him as though He needed us. We all, unless we are stopped, are in danger of taking ourselves too seriously. I am ashamed to think how often I have done this.

What Jesus has done for us at the beginning of the Lord's Prayer is to remind us that we have a Father in heaven, but that He is very different from our human father. It is to remind us to let God be God, that God is wholly "other." He is in heaven; we are on earth. This shows us in one stroke how big He is, how small we are; how much He knows, how little we know.

But the words "in heaven" are not intended to limit God to one area or sphere. God isn't limited to a place called heaven. Solomon said it best: "The heavens, even the highest heaven, cannot contain you" (1 Kings 8:27). Not only that, but God can come alongside us by the Holy Spirit in a hundredth of a second to console us and make us feel special.

By inserting these two words, "in heaven," then, Jesus reminds us of the tenderness of God yet also of His greatness. He reminds us not only of the love of God but of His loftiness; not only of the sweetness of God but of His sovereignty. We certainly do have an *Abba* Father relationship with Him. But we must never outgrow our reverence for Him.

With some relationships, the more you get to know a person the less you truly respect them. I sometimes have people say to me, "I enjoy your preaching. I would love to get to know you better." I then hear myself say in my heart, *Don't spoil it.* But with our heavenly Father, the more you get to know Him the more you respect Him. If, then, you can understand more and more what you are saying when you pray the Lord's Prayer, the more you will respect your heavenly Father. You will come to love, respect, and worship Him for being exactly the way He is.

PART 2

GOD'S PRAYER LIST

CHAPTER 4

PAUSING TO WORSHIP

Hallowed be your name.
—MATTHEW 6:9

THIS IS THE first petition of the Lord's Prayer: "Hallowed be your name," a petition designed such that God may be put in His rightful place by our worship. You could equally conclude that Jesus is keeping us from rushing into God's presence. The most natural tendency in the world when we pray is to turn to God for our wants and wishes—putting forth our requests without any regard for the Father Himself or what may be His agenda.

Another way of putting it: the Lord's Prayer is given to teach us primarily to seek God's face, not His hand. Seeking His hand is to ask Him to "do this" or "do that" for us. Seeking His face is to honor His personhood, His character, His heart, and His own agenda. Most of us think of our own agenda when we pray; it usually does not occur to us that God has an agenda too.

But Jesus knows this. He has given us that greatest prayer ever conceived, and it protects the throne of grace from abuse by our using prayer as a way of getting only what *we* want. Jesus knows that His Father has plans for Himself and a purpose for each of us. Our Lord Jesus therefore has worded this prayer in a manner that focuses on God before we get to our personal wants. It is a God-centered prayer.

Two Halves

Perhaps the best way to understand the Lord's Prayer is to divide it into two halves: God's prayer list and our prayer list. God sets the agenda in both. Does God really have a prayer list? Yes. And the first thing He does is to put His prayer list first. He has three requests: that we pray for (1) His name to be hallowed, (2) His kingdom to come, and (3) His will to be done on earth as it is in heaven.

In a word, the Lord's Prayer gives an immediate invitation to pause and worship before we get to anything else. God wants only what is best for us, and it is best that we learn to focus on God Himself before we focus on our personal needs.

However, keep in mind that Jesus is giving us a pattern for *ideal* praying. As I have said previously, there will be moments when you won't think to recall the pattern of the Lord's Prayer but instead will cry out for help. David apparently did this when he was in exile and felt so helpless with a bleak future. He was low and desperate. He simply prayed, "LORD, turn Ahithophel's counsel into foolishness" (2 Sam. 15:31). And God answered (2 Sam. 17:14). Stephen was being stoned and in great pain just before he died. He simply cried out, "Lord, do not hold this sin against them" (Acts 7:60). God understands this. Our heavenly Father is not imposing the Lord's Prayer on us as an inflexible standard to get His attention. It is a guide, a pattern, a skeleton to help us pray and to know Him.

In a Good Place

If saying "Our Father in heaven" is given to put us in our place, saying "Hallowed be your name," if we pray it from our hearts, demonstrates we are truly *in* our place when we approach God. It means we are in a good place, a very good place indeed. Keep in mind that this prayer is perfectly worded, that the order of the petitions sets a pattern for all praying.

Consider Hebrews 4:16, one of the great verses in the Bible to motivate us to pray: "Let us then approach the throne of grace with confidence, so that we may receive mercy and find grace to help us in our time of need." This verse is also carefully worded and designed to keep us from rushing into God's presence and enumerating our needs before we recognize who He is. It tells us that the first thing we do is *receive mercy* when we approach God.

Does this surprise you? This verse is addressing Christians, not the lost. And yet every Christian, when he or she prays, according to Hebrews 4:16, is to seek God for mercy before we do anything else. Mercy is what the lost sinner requests in order to be accepted by God. The person who is justified before God is the one who prays, "God, have mercy on me, a sinner" (Luke 18:13). And yet Christians are equally told to ask God for mercy when we approach the throne of grace. Why? We never outgrow the need of mercy. Hebrews 4:16 therefore makes us focus on God and His character before anything else. And that is the purpose of this first petition, "Hallowed be your name."

Jesus' Loyalty to the Father

As we pray the Lord's Prayer, we are asked to pause to acknowledge the Father's name. "Don't move on in praying," says Jesus, "until you acknowledge My Father's name." Jesus was eternally loyal to the Father. "The Son can do nothing by himself; he can do only what he sees his Father doing" (John 5:19). His priority was always the Father's name. And now, teaching us how to pray, the first thing He does is teach us also to be loyal to the Father. All that Jesus ever did was with the Father's name in mind. "I have come in my Father's name, and you do not accept me" (John 5:43). "'My food,' said Jesus, 'is to do the will of him who sent me and to finish his work'" (John 4:34). He could say near the close of His earthly ministry, "I have revealed you to those whom you gave me out of the world" (John 17:6).

Talk about loyalty! It is a rare commodity, a rare jewel. You have no way of knowing when you meet a new person or a new friend whether they will be loyal. When you interview someone for a job, or you are looking for someone to work with you, it is virtually impossible to tell whether they will be loyal. Loyalty is what you want in your spouse. It is what a parent wants in their children. It is what a manager wants in his office. It is what any leader or head of state wants of their people. It is what a pastor wants in his church. Jesus was unflinchingly loyal to the Father. Everything Jesus did was to uphold the name of His Father.

Now when Jesus tells us how to pray, He says, as it were, "Before you ask for anything else, say, 'Hallowed be your name.'" The Greek word is from the verb *hagiazo*, "to be holy."[1] The word is used in the imperative passive: "Let your name be hallowed"—or "treated as holy," as John Stott put it. Jesus is not saying, "Holy is your name"; rather, it is a plea that the Father's name be regarded everywhere as holy. Mind you, His name is holy anyway. "Holy and awesome is his name" (Ps. 111:9). "Praise his holy name" (Ps. 103:1). "Whose name is holy" (Isa. 57:15). This petition therefore is not a plea that His name become holy but that His name be *seen* as holy.

We must ask ourselves a question: Do *we* regard the Father's name as holy? In this petition we are made to pause, to acknowledge that name which, according to Paul, is "above every name" (Phil. 2:9). How can we ask that this name be hallowed if we ourselves do not treat His name as holy? We therefore are to be still, to think, to ponder this name. We do not merely approach the Father; we are to acknowledge His name.

What's in a Name?

There are two essential things in a name: identity and reputation. "Moses said to God, 'Suppose I go to the Israelites and say to them, "The God of your fathers has sent me to you," and they ask me, "What is his name?" Then what shall I tell them?' God said to Moses, '"I AM WHO I AM. This is what you are to say to the Israelites: "I AM has sent me to you"'" (Exod. 3:13–14). The name *Yahweh* means "I am who I am," or "I will be who I will be." That is God's name, which identifies the God of Israel.

In ancient times a person's name was closely related to what he or she is; the name was often explanatory and revelatory. The name Abraham, for example, means "father of many nations" (Gen. 17:5). The name Israel means "he struggles with God." (See Genesis 32:28.) Shakespeare asked, "What's in a name?" but certainly he did not take biblical names seriously when he said, "A rose by any other name would smell as sweet."[2] For God's name could only be *Yahweh*.

A name also is tied to one's reputation. "A good name is more desirable than great riches; to be esteemed is better than silver or gold" (Prov. 22:1). Moses appealed to God's name and reputation when he interceded for Israel. The Lord told Moses He was going to destroy the people of Israel for their unbelief and start all over with Moses to build a new nation. But Moses said, "No!" "Then the Egyptians will hear about it! By your power you brought these people up from among them....If you put all these people to death, leaving none alive, the nations who have heard this report about you will say, 'The LORD [*Yahweh*] was not able to bring these people into the land he promised them on oath'" (Num. 14:13, 15–16). Moses thus appealed to God's great name—both His identity and reputation—and asked that God forgive the people instead. God did (Num. 14:20).

Joshua interceded in the same way, fearing what enemy nations would think if God did not show mercy and intervene. Joshua asked, "What then will you do for your own great name?" (Josh. 7:9). The name of God was of paramount importance in ancient Israel. "Ascribe to the LORD the glory due his name" (1 Chron. 16:29). David's chief motive in wanting to build the temple was for "the Name of the LORD my God" (1 Kings 5:5). God said, "I have chosen Jerusalem for my Name to be there" (2 Chron. 6:6). What an honor for a city! What a reputation to maintain!

The Lord's Prayer should be prayed with earnest and tearful zeal that the name of the Lord be hallowed, that it be treated as holy. Both the identity and reputation of God's name are meant when we pray this petition. I appeal to all who read these lines: learn to respect the Father's name; pray that you will have a deep conviction and jealousy with regard to the name of the Lord. Pray that you will be grieved when His name is desecrated.

Participating in the Father's Name

To pray this first petition means to participate in the mystique and glory of the Father's name: the LORD, *Yahweh*. It is such a privilege to do so. God might even have kept us from knowing it. You could suggest that it is because Moses put God on the spot, as it were, that we even know His name (Exod. 3:13). God actually went for centuries without revealing His name to the patriarchs. He told Moses, "I appeared to Abraham, to Isaac and to Jacob as God Almighty, but by my name the LORD [*Yahweh*] I did not make myself fully known to them" (Exod. 6:3).

Why is the name of the Lord awesome? It is because nobody else could have that name: *I* AM *that I* AM. Only God has no beginning. "From everlasting to everlasting you are God" (Ps. 90:2). Every child asks, "Where did God come from? Who made God?" The answer is ever the same: *God always was and is.* There is no more staggering thought. He always was; He never had a beginning. No brilliant intellect can fathom this. All we can do is take off our shoes, for we are on holy ground. We have been given the privilege of participating in the divine nature (2 Pet. 1:4). How do we participate in the glory and mystique of the Father's name? For one thing, by carefully pausing to acknowledge His name. By being guarded when we speak (Ps. 141:3). By admitting we are out of our depth. By realizing it is such a privilege.

By praise and adoration. And now, with some knowledge of God's identity—and concern for His reputation—we can pray the Lord's Prayer with more care.

We must learn to praise and adore the name of our Father and Jesus' Father by our lips. "Not to us, LORD, not to us but to your name be the glory, because of your love and faithfulness" (Ps. 115:1). "Glorify the LORD with me; let us exalt his name together" (Ps. 34:3). We do this when speaking, when witnessing, and in times of public prayer, as when those who feared the Lord "talked with each other, and the LORD listened and heard" (Mal. 3:16). Not only that, "A scroll of remembrance was written in his presence concerning those who feared the LORD and honored his name" (Mal. 3:16). We do it when singing: "Sing to the LORD a new song; sing to the LORD, all the earth. Sing to the LORD, praise his name" (Ps. 96:1–2). We do this when we pray, as did the Israelites in Nehemiah's day when they said, "Blessed be your glorious name, and may it be exalted above all blessing and praise" (Neh. 9:5).

We show deference to God's name by our conversation. I have said that my most "unfavorite" verse in the Bible is when Jesus said, "But I tell you that everyone will have to give account on the day of judgment for every empty word they have spoken" (Matt. 12:36). If that is true—and it is—the continual awareness of the honor of God's name will help me to be more guarded when I speak. We honor God's name by speaking blessings, as when Paul said, "Let your conversation be always full of grace, seasoned with salt, so that you may know how to answer everyone" (Col. 4:6). What would our conversation be like if Jesus were physically present with us? Well, He certainly is present by the person of the Holy Spirit!

We honor our Father's name by our loyalty. That is the point I made earlier. Jesus was utterly loyal to the Father. Were we to become jealous for the honor of God's name, we would be mirroring the person and likeness of Jesus to a very great measure. There is a godly jealousy that extols God's name (2 Cor. 11:2).

We Make a Pledge

When we pray, "Hallowed be your name," it is a pledge to be accountable to that name. Accountability is when you are obliged to give a reckoning or explanation for your actions. If I pray for God's name to be treated as holy, yet have no regard for manifesting holiness in my own life, I am a hypocrite. I therefore regard my prayer for God's name to be hallowed as a commitment to be the kind of person who brings glory to God's name. We all are accountable to the Father for our actions; my prayer that His name be treated as holy will be applied by my sincere effort to honor His name by my personal life.

I must be careful never to abuse or misuse the name of God. The third commandment, "You shall not misuse the name of the LORD your God" (Exod. 20:7), is vast and far more profound than many suppose. It certainly means I must not use profanity and that I never say things like "Oh, God" in anger. But that is the bare beginning of understanding the third commandment. Jesus taught the fuller meaning of this in the Sermon on the Mount (Matt. 5:33–37). This includes dragging God's name into our personal interests— as in a pet doctrine or project—and claiming to have God's backing for what we stand for. We all want to believe that God is on "our" side. When we use His name as we would a respected person to support our point of view, we misuse that precious name. It is not right to pray that God's name be treated as holy and then turn around and use His name to endorse my enterprise so others will endorse it too. Not only that, when I say, "The Lord told me this," chances are I am not trying to make *Him* look good but to make *myself* look good. That is misusing His name. To pray "Hallowed be your name" is to embrace and live the meaning of the prophet's word, "I am the LORD; that is my name! I will not yield my glory to another" (Isa. 42:8).

Therefore, when I pray, "Hallowed be your name," it is not something I utter with my mouth only; it is like a pledge—a solemn promise—to put this into practice. Praying the Lord's Prayer is not something you are called to do by praying it and then forgetting about it; praying it is a reminder to put it into practice, as we shall see with all the petitions. Praying this petition is a pledge to treat God's name as holy since you are His child; you represent Him in the world, and you are the nearest some people will ever come to seeing the Father's face.

But there is more. To pray "Hallowed be your name" is to pray for the advancement of the reputation of the Father's name. You are thus praying that the Father's name will be held in the honor it deserves so that people may never think of Him without highest reverence. It is our prayer that the whole world will bow before God.

You can certainly apply this prayer to your own church. Would you not like God to put His name on your church as He did Jerusalem? What greater honor can there be? Pray then that God will esteem your church to the degree He is pleased to put His name there. Why? Because His reputation is at stake—and He knows that your church upholds

His name, which is why He would not be ashamed to put His name there.

Does God Need Prayer?

This first petition of the Lord's Prayer is therefore like a prayer request from God that He Himself will grant that His name be hallowed. You might overlook what is obvious: this is God's own request! It is God's request that we pray for the honor of His name to be evident on the earth. It may seem ironic. Should you pray for God? Does He need prayer? Not quite. But in this case He wants us to participate in the advancement of His glory. He could in one second cause the whole world to hallow His name. But He has chosen instead to ask us to participate in a huge process. We therefore pray to Him that He will see to it that His name be treated as holy. It is not unlike praying that He will manifest His glory, for God's glory and His name are inseparable.

It is summed up well by the prophet Ezekiel: "I will show the holiness of my great name, which has been profaned among the nations, the name you have profaned among them. Then the nations will know that I am the LORD, declares the Sovereign LORD, when I am proved holy through you before their eyes" (Ezek. 36:23).

Finally, if God does not seem to respond to our prayer, "Hallowed be your name," we continue to pray anyway, "Hallowed be your name." It is one thing to worship when He is pleasing us and coming through every day by answering our requests; it is another to worship when He isn't doing exactly what we want. The Lord can give or take away; "may the name of the LORD be praised" (Job 1:21). Or, as the three Hebrew young men put it when they were threatened with the possibility of a burning fiery furnace: "If we are thrown into the blazing furnace, the God we serve is able to deliver us from it....But *even if he does not*, we want you to know, Your Majesty, that we will not serve your gods or worship the image of gold you have set up" (Dan. 3:17–18, emphasis mine).

Do not forget that the Father's name is holy already. He is holy in Himself. His name is all that is true of God, for God's name is what He is. But we pray that this will be demonstrated in *our* lives, whether all of those around us bow to God or not. The first petition of the Lord's Prayer therefore is a call to worship—to worship God for being just as He is.

CHAPTER 5

FOCUSING ON GOD'S INTEREST

Your kingdom come.
—MATTHEW 6:10

J ONATHAN EDWARDS (1703–1758), the greatest theologian
in American history, taught us that one of the things the
devil cannot do is produce in us a love for God's interest
and glory. Satan is a great counterfeiter. But he cannot put
in your heart an unfeigned concern for what concerns God.

Why is this important? For one thing, if you have a love
for God's glory, it shows you have been genuinely converted.
I take the view that the primary basis of assurance of salvation is to look to Jesus Christ, who died on the cross for our
sins. If you trust Him—not your works—you are saved. But
there are some who feel they have done this and yet worry
whether they have been saved. If so, Edwards' teaching provides a secondary ground of assurance. If you love God's
glory and what interests *Him*, you can be sure you have
crossed over from death into life; Satan did not put that love
there. He is indeed a great counterfeiter, but he is simply
unable to make you focus freely on God's concerns.

In giving us the second petition of the Lord's Prayer—
"Your kingdom come"—Jesus further turns our attention to
what interests God. Most of us care about what interests
us—our needs, our wants, our wishes. We are living in the
Me Generation—"What's in it for me?" So much preaching,
teaching, and theologizing today is man-centered. Much
praying is man-centered. It wasn't always like that, but I'm
afraid it is now. And it's getting worse.

Jesus makes us focus on God. He does it at the beginning of the prayer, not the end. It is the opposite of the way
too many of us pray. We turn to God and start enumerating
our requests, and then at the end, just maybe, we say, "And
we will give You all the praise for what You do"—and that
is about as much focus as God gets. When you realize that
God wants only what is best for us, you should know also
it is best for us to learn to focus on God before we focus on
ourselves. Doing things His way is always best.

We have seen that God has a prayer list of His own, and
He puts His requests right at the beginning of this remark-
able prayer. First on God's prayer list is that we will pray
that His name be treated as holy on the planet He has made.
His second request is that we pray for the coming of His
kingdom. God did not have to unveil His wish for how we
should pray. I have long been amazed at what He communicated through the psalmist. Having said that He owns the
cattle on a thousand hills, He added, "If I were hungry *I
would not tell you*, for the world is mine, and all that is in
it" (Ps. 50:12, emphasis mine). And yet here He asks us to
pray for the honor of His name and for the coming of His
kingdom.

Focusing on God Is in Our Best Interest

Why does Jesus reveal the Father's heart in this candid way? *It is for us.* He would do us no favor to let us carry on with a preoccupation of self-interest. When we become full of ourselves and keep putting our personal requests to God all the time, we set ourselves up for more selfishness and self-pity, which gets us nowhere. The best thing our Father could do for us is to require us to meditate on Him. Are you depressed at the moment? Are you worried? Has everything suddenly gone wrong for you? What if you were thrown into prison, like Paul and Silas, for doing the right thing? In the middle of the night they began singing praises and hymns to God. I for one would love to see a replay of that scene when we get to heaven! While they were singing, a violent earthquake shook the foundations of the prison. The result was that the jailer and his family were converted (Acts 16:25–34).

We had a Sunday afternoon prayer meeting each week at Westminster Chapel prior to the evening service. I decided one day to get the group to postpone putting a request to God, but only to *thank Him* for things. It was slow getting started. We are in such a habit of putting forth our requests, even valid ones. But I kept the people from asking for anything for fifteen minutes each week—and then we could ask for things. Never forget Paul's exhortation: "Do not be anxious about anything, but in every situation, by prayer and petition, *with thanksgiving*, present your requests to God" (Phil. 4:6, emphasis mine).

Thanksgiving takes discipline on our part. It takes effort. This is why the writer of Hebrews refers to "a sacrifice of praise" (Heb. 13:15). In much the same way, our prayer of "Hallowed be your name, your kingdom come, your will be

63

done on earth as it is in heaven" lifts us out of ourselves to participate in God's concerns. This approach not only honors Him but is good for us, to get our eyes off ourselves. Not only that, but it will lift your spirit. Try singing hymns when all hell is breaking out. God may send an earthquake and turn you into a soul winner! When Paul had some time on his hands in Athens, he decided to go to the marketplace to witness to those who "happened to be there" (Acts 17:17). This led to what was arguably the most prestigious invitation Paul ever got—to address the philosophers at the Areopagus. It would be like giving a talk to the faculty at Oxford or Cambridge. Paul did not engineer the invitation; it fell into his lap. And all because Paul used his time to focus on God's interest.

In the Lord's Prayer, God lets us share in His own heartbeat. It is such a privilege. You and I are invited to partake in the greatest enterprise in all creation: the reason God sent His Son into the world in the first place. Talk about getting significance! There is no higher calling, no greater goal, no greater mission. You are I are given a mandate to pray for that which is greater than politics, greater than economic success, greater than national security: that God's kingdom may come. It doesn't get better than that.

The Message of Jesus

The first message of Jesus was, "Repent, for the kingdom of heaven has come near" (Matt. 4:17; see also Mark 1:15). The opening sentence in the Sermon on the Mount is, "Blessed are the poor in spirit, for theirs is the kingdom of heaven" (Matt. 5:3). When Jesus told us to pray "Your kingdom come," it meant asking God to *actualize*—that is, to let us *experience*—what He had been talking about up to that point in the Sermon on the Mount. In other words, what Jesus had said was "near," or at hand, was now to be made real, actual.

However, the kingdom of heaven that Jesus had in mind was vastly different from what the disciples hoped it would be. It is unlikely they grasped the meaning Jesus intended. Even after His resurrection they could not get out of their mindset that Jesus had come to set up His kingdom (Acts 1:6). They thought it would be visible, victorious, and exalt Israel over all other nations, especially Rome. Wrong. The kingdom of God "is not something that can be observed," Jesus would later say, because the "kingdom of God is in your midst" (Luke 17:21). This coheres with all Jesus said about the kingdom in the Sermon on the Mount and further shows what Jesus meant by our praying, "Your kingdom come." Although the kingdom of God can also be described in eschatological terms—meaning the second coming—Jesus clearly meant what is invisible, not what is visible. The kingdom of God takes place *in the heart*.

The highest privilege and the greatest joy on earth is consciously being in God's kingdom. Jesus said it comes through brokenness (Matt. 5:3), persecution (vv. 11–12), and exceeding the righteousness of the Pharisees (v. 20). And yet we are told in the Lord's Prayer to *pray* for it to come.

Question: Do you want the kingdom of God to come? If so, would you believe that God the Father wants it to come more than you do? What should be most important to us—the wish for the kingdom to come—is most important to God. God was grieved when ancient Israel asked for a king, to be like other nations. "I am...your king," God would say to them (Isa. 43:15). But God gave in to their request and ordered Samuel to let them have their own way: "Listen to all that the people are saying to you; it is not you they have rejected, but they have rejected me as their king" (1 Sam. 8:7). I think of that scary verse in Psalm 106:15: God gave them their request "but sent leanness into their soul" (KJV). Never forget too that the prophet would say later on: "In my anger I gave you a king, and in my wrath I took him away" (Hos. 13:11). God Himself was their king, but God being their king was not enough for them; they wanted to be like other nations.

What God wanted was that He Himself would dwell in the hearts of the people of Israel, to reign over them and rule in them. This is exactly what Jesus came to proclaim—that the Most High God, who inhabits eternity, would live in the hearts of His people. But for the disciples to grasp this perspective meant a paradigm shift, a changing of gears, a radical readjustment in their perception. They were looking for the nation of Israel to be put back on the map.

Grasping the Meaning of the Kingdom of God

What exactly did Jesus mean by "the kingdom"? There are several definitions that could be basically right. First, the fundamental meaning of the phrase "kingdom of God" is simply the realm of God's domain. This realm is called a kingdom because God alone is sovereign in it. His realm is in heaven, and He reigns there. There is no rebellion to His will in heaven; He has no competition there, no rival. Heaven was emptied of all revolt a long time ago (2 Pet. 2:4; Jude 6). God is worshipped there by all the angelic creation as well as all the believers who have died. But His kingdom extends to the earth as well. His presence inhabits the whole of His creation, although "we do not yet see everything in subjection to him" here below (Heb. 2:8, ESV). But one day that will change; every knee will bow before Jesus Christ and every tongue confess Him as Lord and King (Rom. 14:11; Phil. 2:9–11). This will be the ultimate manifestation of God's kingdom. This is partly what Jesus means when we pray, "Your kingdom come."

However, the chief meaning of "kingdom" in the Lord's Prayer is what Jesus meant by it in His teaching, as revealed in the Sermon on the Mount. The kingdom is the immediate, direct, and conscious witness of the Holy Spirit. It is *God's conscious presence and enabling grace*. Jesus primarily meant *the rule of the ungrieved, unquenched Spirit in our hearts*. The plea "Your kingdom come" was actually meant in Matthew 7:7: "Ask and it will be given to you; seek and you will find; knock and the door will be opened to you." Jesus said this in the Sermon on the Mount when, had His hearers been grasping what He was teaching, they would be hungry for God Himself. The Sermon on the Mount should make one thirsty for God. Jesus said if we are hungry and thirsty for righteousness, we will be filled (Matt. 5:6). If His hearers (or readers, in our case) took in what Jesus had been saying up to that point, then Matthew 7:7 would appeal to those who are hungry and thirsty for God. Whereas Matthew 7:11 promises "good gifts" to those who ask, the parallel account in Luke 11:13, also following the Lord's Prayer (Luke 11:2–4), inserts "Holy Spirit." Read the two accounts alongside each other (Matt. 7:7–11 and Luke 11:9–13) and you will see this.

The kingdom Jesus describes simply comes to this: the Holy Spirit. After Jesus died, rose again, and ascended to the right hand of God, a broader meaning of the kingdom emerged: the second coming. The two men in white said to the disciples as they looked at the clouds into which the ascending Jesus disappeared, "This same Jesus, who has been taken from you into heaven, will come back in the same way you have seen him go into heaven" (Acts 1:11). Paul also referred to the kingdom as meaning the second coming when he said Jesus will judge the living and the dead "in view of his appearing and his kingdom" (2 Tim. 4:1). The point being, when Jesus comes again, He will come in great power and glory, and the kingdom of God will mean the defeat of all evil (1 Cor. 15:24–28). This is understanding the kingdom in an eschatological sense. Not only that, but we have a perfect right to interpret "Your kingdom come" in the Lord's Prayer to mean the second coming. We say with John, "Come, Lord Jesus" (Rev. 22:20). It is perfectly right to pray for the second coming when you pray the Lord's Prayer.

However, I do not think this is what Jesus primarily meant at the time He was presenting the Lord's Prayer to His followers. Yes, we certainly can wish for the second coming when we pray the Lord's Prayer. But both in the Sermon on the Mount and Luke 11:3–13, the kingdom is to be understood in terms of the Spirit, and we do well to apply it in that manner. If we think of the kingdom as being only eschatological and futuristic, we will miss a great deal of what Jesus meant then—and what God wants to do now in all of us.

To interpret the kingdom of God to mean only the future is to make the Sermon on the Mount basically irrelevant at the present time. It lets us off the hook and makes such righteousness unnecessary. I believe the Sermon on the Mount is to be lived *in the here and now*. The kingdom was taught by Jesus as being the kind of experience God wants for His people—now—*before* Jesus comes again. This means experiencing an internal righteousness that exceeds the righteousness of the Pharisees, which was only an external righteousness. What Jesus was teaching was utterly alien to the Pharisees. For example: having no hatred in the heart but rather blessing your enemy (Matt. 5:21–22, 43–48), no lusting (5:27–30), giving and praying to be seen only by God (6:1–8). Therefore, when Jesus told us to pray, "Your kingdom come," He meant inviting the Holy Spirit to so dwell in us that we demonstrate the very righteousness Jesus has preached. We also simultaneously pray for the second coming of Jesus when we say, "Your kingdom come." Yes, we have it both ways.

The Paradox Regarding God's Kingdom

But there is a paradox in understanding the kingdom of God. The kingdom of God has been established by Jesus, and yet we nonetheless pray for it to come. God is sovereign and in complete control. So we do not pray for Him to be our sovereign, our monarch, our king. He already is. Jesus now reigns at the right hand of God. Yet we pray for His kingdom to come, that it will become apparent in our hearts—and in the world, that all will know that Jesus Christ is Lord. This is a recurring theme in Ezekiel: "And so I will show my greatness and my holiness, and I will make myself known in the sight of many nations. Then they will know that I am the LORD" (Ezek. 38:23). And yet when we pray for the second coming, this is what we are hoping for.

There is a second paradox: the open declaration that we all see Jesus Christ is coming anyway, and yet we pray for it. This will happen on a date already set by God the Father

(Matt. 24:36). Nothing can stop this. But why pray for it? I can give two reasons. First, if John Wesley is basically right, that God does nothing but in answer to prayer, we should pray for the second coming. Secondly, there is a sense in which we may speed the day of His coming (2 Pet. 3:11–12). God is sovereign in all His timing. But—and don't try to figure it out—prayer makes things happen.

There is actually a third paradox. Praying for the kingdom to come is an unselfish request—it focuses on God's interest—yet it is in our own interest to pray this. It is unselfish in that we rise above our personal requests and pray for God's greater glory. We see sin and rebellion in society; poverty and hunger; corruption in politics and business; millions of abortions; evil and suffering; a world that does not know God; a world that hates God. We long for God to be glorified and recognized. And yet to pray, "Your kingdom come," becomes almost selfish. The Holy Spirit will give us a love for God's interest and glory, and we might even get carried away with wanting God's honor. It becomes a part of you; you can't tell whether it is a natural or spiritual desire, whether it is what God wants or what you want, because you want it so much. "Come, Lord Jesus."

What is the purpose in praying for God's kingdom to come? Why focus on God's interest? The answer is, partly, that we will get our eyes off ourselves. As we have said, before bringing our personal requests, we focus on God and what is His burden. God is the most maligned person in the universe, the most unvindicated person who ever was or is. I want to be around when God clears His own name. He looks forward to it too. So let us make every effort to get our eyes off ourselves and our personal vindication and seek God's.

There are two things further I want to mention in this chapter: first, the ungrieved Spirit. This is what I mean: the Holy Spirit is a very sensitive person and can be grieved (Eph. 4:30). When He is grieved, it is as if the dove (a New Testament symbol of the Spirit) gets frightened and flies away. Not that the Holy Spirit utterly leaves us—no, that is not the case. But we temporarily lose the blessing of the Spirit—the anointing. When the Holy Spirit is grieved, the anointing lifts from us; when the Holy Spirit is not grieved—and the Spirit is Himself—the anointing enables us to do what had been utterly impossible. This is why I said earlier that the kingdom is the rule of the ungrieved Spirit, and that is precisely what we pray for when we say, "Your kingdom come."

Second, there is the silent divorce in the church between the Word and the Spirit. I believe the Word and the Spirit will be remarried and that the simultaneous combination will result in spontaneous combustion. This will bring the kingdom of God in power like our generation has not seen. Therefore, when you pray, "Your kingdom come," it is most fitting to pray that the kingdom will come in this apostolic power—as in the Book of Acts.

I urge you to pray for this. I believe this will happen before the second coming, resulting in power to the church that is unprecedented since the days of the early church. I believe the blindness on Israel will be lifted, resulting in countless thousands of Jews coming to see Jesus as their Messiah. I believe Islam will be penetrated by the gospel and millions of Arabs will be converted to Jesus Christ. All this will come as a result of the Word and Spirit coming together as in the earliest church.

To pray "Your kingdom come" is to pray for the success of

the gospel. It is to be raised above our own personal needs for a moment. Focus on God—His prayer requests. What God wants is always what is best for us. What began as an effort, a discipline, and a sacrifice—putting our needs to one side—ends up as a blessing: being filled with the Holy Spirit and an experience of the kingdom of God that Jesus had in mind all along.

CHAPTER 6

WANTING WHAT GOD WANTS

Your will be done, on earth as it is in heaven.
—MATTHEW 6:10

THIS IS THE third petition of the Lord's Prayer—you could say God's third "prayer request"—but it is all for us. In any case, before we are allowed to turn to our personal situation in the Lord's Prayer, we are particularly blessed with an invitation to pray for God's will.

I am so glad this petition is there. The sweetest place in the world to be is in the will of God. I would rather have this than anything; I would rather pray for this than anything. What a privilege to pray like this. How wonderful that God wants this for us.

The most thrilling thing to me is that (1) God has a will of His own and (2) He wants us to participate in it. This petition militates against a theological perspective that has been in vogue for a few years called "open theism." It is deadly. But open theism has caught on with a surprising number of people. The idea is that God has no definite will of His own but cooperates with us; we and God are in it together; He gets input from us to know what to do next. Not only that, but there is no guarantee God will be victorious at the end of the day if you take this perspective seriously. He could lose in the end. Wrong. God losing is not possible.

Not only does God have a will of His own, but our Lord instructs us to acknowledge His will before we move on. The fact that Jesus said to pray, "Your will be done," shows that God has a will, an opinion.

There is an inseparable connection between the will of God and the glory of God. The root word of the Greek *doxa* (glory), from which we get *doxology*, means "opinion."[1] The heart of the glory of God is God's opinion. I once wrote a catechism for a church I pastored in Oxfordshire before coming to London, and in it I defined the glory of God as the "dignity of His will." There is nothing greater, nothing wiser, nothing safer, nothing nobler, nothing better than the will of God. For the will of God reveals His glory.

Has it occurred to you that God has an opinion on the matter confronting you at the moment? Do you realize that God has an opinion as to what is going on in the world today? Do you not know that God has an opinion on what you should do next?

I, for one, want His opinion. Don't you? Of course you do.

You honor a person by asking for their opinion, their wisdom. I ask for people's opinions all the time. I had a number of friends read the manuscript of this book before it was published. Why? Because in a multitude of advisers there is safety (Prov. 11:14). I want to get it right. My greatest fear is that I would accept and teach error.

Therefore, when Jesus tells us to pray, "Your will be done," the assumption is that the Father already has an opinion. His opinion is what lies behind His will. Jesus takes this for granted. This is really no great revelation, that God has a will. It is merely that I have learned to appreciate this fact the older I get.

So what Jesus requests of us is that we acknowledge that God has a will. We don't inform Him of what His will ought to be. We only want Him to have His way. *"Your will be done."* We don't want anything to stop His will from being perfectly carried out. We respect His opinion; we want it carried out.

By mentioning the Father's *will*, then, Jesus shows that (1) God is independent from us and has a will of His own without our input, and (2) God thinks for Himself; He has a mind of His own. In a word: God has a plan. It is an architectural blueprint drawn up from the foundation of the world. Long before we were born, long before our parents were born, long before their parents were born, long before Adam and Eve were created in the Garden of Eden, long before there was ever a tree, a blade of grass, or a star, God had a plan. "I make known the end from the beginning, from ancient times, what is still to come. I say, 'My purpose will stand, and I will do all that I please'" (Isa. 46:10). "When I was woven together in the depths of the earth. Your eyes saw my unformed body; all the days ordained for me were written in your book before one of them came to be" (Ps. 139:15–16).

The Revealed Will of God

One of the main things I learned from studying the Puritan William Perkins (1558–1602) at Oxford was that the will of God is to be understood in two ways: (1) His *revealed will* and (2) His *secret will*. The revealed will of God is, simply, the Bible. The Bible includes sixty-six books, thirty-nine in the Old Testament, twenty-seven in the New Testament. The Old Testament is generally comprised of the Law (the first five books), the Psalms, and the Prophets. But there are also books of poetry and historical books. The New Testament is generally comprised of the teachings of Jesus and letters, mostly from the apostle Paul.

Do you want to know the will of God? Read the Bible! That is the best, most God-honoring way to know His will. It is caring enough about Him to read what He has said. As the hymn put it, "What more can be said than to you God hath said?"[2] I don't mean to be unfair, but you probably get to know God's will largely in proportion to how much you actually love God—that is, love His revealed will, His written Word.

Sadly, most people want a shortcut to God's will. Reading the Bible takes too long! They want to know *right now* what they should do. But the truth is, the more you know the Bible the more you know His will. You get to know God basically one way: *by spending time with Him.* And this is done basically two ways: reading the Bible and praying. When you spend time each day praying and reading your Bible, you are going to get to know God more and more! That's a guarantee.

A friend of mine who is known for his prophetic gift told me how he gets tired of dozens of people coming up to him every five minutes, asking, "Do you have a word for me?" One evening in church a lady asked him again, "Do you have a word for me?" He was angry (although fortunately the lady didn't know it) and handed her his own Bible and said, "Yes, I have a word for you—read this!" She took it as a word from God. When the same man with the prophetic gift returned to that church two years later, everyone said this lady knew the Bible more than anybody in town! She had taken his word as a *rhema* word, which I will now describe.

There are at least two Greek words translated "word": *logos* and *rhema*. Although you cannot push the distinctions too far (because sometimes they overlap), there has been a craze in recent years for a "rhema" word—known as a prophetic word, a word of knowledge, a direct word from God on what to do next. You hear it on Christian television all the time: "Don't change the channel! Stay tuned and receive a rhema word!" This is what so many people want. In the day of fast foods—McDonald's and Kentucky Fried Chicken (which I confess I enjoy!)—too many of us want a *quick word* from God because we are too busy to read the Bible. I don't think He likes that very much. You esteem God's glory more by seeking His will in His Word than by focusing on a rhema word. I do believe God gives an immediate word on occasion; I have had that happen, for which I am most grateful. But by and large, the best way to know God's will is to know His Word so well that you hardly need to want anything more than this.

The Secret Will of God

This refers to the details of His plans that He conceived before creation. This aspect of God's will is vast and profound. It refers to His infinite wisdom, His unrevealed plans for us, where we will be five years from now, who will be saved, the exact date of the second coming, whom one should marry, what your career should be, where you should live, when the Holy Spirit will come in unprecedented power.

The secret will of God is what is meant when the prophet

says, "My thoughts are not your thoughts, neither are your ways my ways" (Isa. 55:8). Paul was referring largely to God's secret will when he said, "In him we were also chosen, having been predestined according to the plan of him who works out everything in conformity with the purpose of his will" (Eph. 1:11). Mind you, it is the *revealed* will here (Paul's word) that shows there is a *secret* will. The trouble is, we tend to seek out what God's *secret* will is before we get to know His *revealed* will.

A rhema word usually refers to God's secret will. In June 1970 God gave me a rhema word, showing Louise and me in a second—clearly, absolutely, and unmistakably—that we were to resign our church in Fort Lauderdale and complete my theological education, which eventually led us to England. There was never a doubt in my mind from that moment. However, that sort of thing does not come every day.

The secret will of God is linked to predestination. For example, "This man [Jesus] was handed over to you by God's deliberate plan and foreknowledge" (Acts 2:23). "They [Pontius Pilate and those who crucified Jesus] did what your [God's] power and will had decided beforehand should happen" (Acts 4:28). "All who were appointed for eternal life believed" (Acts 13:48). It is God's revealed will that tells us that God has a secret will.

Sometimes the two overlap. When Ananias informed Paul, "The God of our ancestors has chosen you to know his will" (Acts 22:14), it was a reference to God's secret will for Paul. But knowing what God's will was in Acts 22:17–21 meant God's revealed will. Ananias actually meant that the Holy Spirit was going to reveal the truth of God's Word to Paul, which he had not grasped before. I can think of no greater gift than for God to reveal the knowledge of His will—the Bible—to me. My greatest aspiration is to understand the Bible.

I suppose the secret will of God is more interesting, more compelling, more exciting, and sometimes more sensational than the revealed will. Getting an undoubted word of knowledge is easier than hours and hours of wrestling with God in reading the Bible and praying. But the latter should be our immediate and fundamental search; the secret will of God will be clear to you when you need to know it. Seek to know the secret will of God as a primary focus and it will elude you; aspire to know the revealed will of God and you will gain the general knowledge of His will—and receive a rhema word when you aren't expecting it.

The more you seek to know God's revealed will, the more you will see His secret will unfolded. Paul was determined to go to Asia because he was obeying God's revealed will (to preach the gospel to every person). But to his surprise, he was kept by the Holy Spirit from preaching the Word in the province of Asia (Acts 16:7). The revealed will would mean, "Go to Asia." But the secret will said, "Stop—don't go to Asia." This could only mean that God would have someone else go to Asia—or that Paul would do it later on. But not then.

The Will of God in the Lord's Prayer

When Jesus told us to pray, "Your will be done," did He mean God's revealed will or His secret will? Answer: both. We pray that the truth of God as revealed in Scripture will be carried out on this earth. We equally pray that all God has planned for us will be carried out, in His time. It is a prayer for both the success of what God has promised in His Word and the execution of all His purposes in the world.

When you pray, "Your will be done," it also means you *accept* His will. When you say, "Your will be done," you affirm His revealed will (Scripture); you also accept what He has willed (the unfolding of His plans). When Paul could not be persuaded to avoid going to Jerusalem, everyone acquiesced, saying, "The Lord's will be done," although they were not very happy about it (Acts 21:14). Job said, "The LORD gave and the LORD has taken away; may the name of the LORD be praised" (Job 1:21).

Accepting God's will means that you approve of it, you honor it. Not that you are always thrilled to your fingertips, but you dignify His will. Why? You *want what God wants*. We all must follow Jesus to Gethsemane. There Jesus prayed, "Father, if you are willing, take this cup from me; yet not my will, but yours be done" (Luke 22:42). If we know what God wants, we say, "Yes." If we don't know what God wants, we sign a blank check. I write my name at the appropriate place and say to God, "You fill it out."

Dignifying God's will shows our love for His glory. The glory of God is the dignity of His will; we show we love His glory by dignifying His will—approving it, wanting what God wants.

And yet when we pray, "Your will be done," we are *appealing* for God to carry out His will. Whatever God has in mind, we say, "Do it." The sooner the better, "Your will be done." It means surrendering to His will, surrendering our so-called rights (which we thought were ours). It means surrendering to His plan and wishes. It is like the hymn put it, "My ambitions, plans, and wishes, at my feet in ashes lay."[3]

It is not always easy to know the next step forward in

knowing the secret will of God. In the Old Testament, people would cast lots. This is how the tribes of Israel knew where to settle (Josh. 18:10). Gideon put out his fleece to know for sure he was hearing God (Judg. 6:39–40). The *urim* and *thummim* (when the priest would reach into his pouch and pull up a white stone or black stone) were used to know the will of God. A white stone meant yes, a black stone, no—or something like this let the priest know what to do.

In the New Testament, the way forward to know the will of God was to know the Word of God so well and be so filled with the Spirit that you had clear guidance. Dr. Martyn Lloyd-Jones used to say that the Bible was not given to replace the miraculous; it was given to correct abuses. Therefore, we may have the kind of relationship with God that we know His Word backward and forward, but also know the Holy Spirit in such a manner that we can sense His yes and no. We read that the Holy Spirit said to Philip, "Go to that chariot and stay near it" (Acts 8:29). This intimacy and obedience led to the conversion of the Ethiopian eunuch. God can do that today too.

The Accomplishment of God's Will on Earth

What we want to see, then, is the *accomplishment* of God's will. "Your will be done, on earth as it is in heaven" (Matt. 6:10). We pray that God's will shall be accomplished on earth without any resistance. *The will of God is being done perfectly in heaven*. There is no rebellion in heaven. There will be no more revolts in heaven (Jude 6; 2 Pet. 2:4). All the angels that remain are elect angels (1 Tim. 5:21). The Lord's Prayer therefore gives us a mandate to pray that God's will on earth will be carried out as perfectly as it is in heaven. All the inhabitants of heaven worship God without any constraint or reluctance. The angels, the cherubim, the seraphim, and those with the Lord (Heb. 12:23) are all worshipping God with total freedom.

Our prayer, then, is that God's will in heaven will be mirrored on earth, without any interference, reluctance, or rebellion. But should we pray for what will never be accomplished until the end of the world? Yes. Jesus' high priestly prayer is not fully answered yet: "My prayer is not for them alone. I pray also for those who will believe in me through their message, that all of them may be one, Father, just as you are in me and I am in you. May they also be in us so that the world may believe that you have sent me" (John 17:20–21). So yes, we keep praying for that which is not answered yet.

But what can we fully wish for now? I should pray that, as far as we are concerned, there will be no revolt left in us, no rebellion in us, no stubbornness in us, no reluctance in us. I can't answer for the world; I can't answer for you. I can answer for myself. I want God's will to be carried out in me as perfectly as it is being carried out in heaven.

Some people take the view that this prayer is a mandate for people's healing. The view is that there is no sickness in heaven; therefore, we should ask God to heal people and expect them to be as it is in heaven. Nice thought. But I don't think that is the meaning. There is no evil in heaven, either. Evil will remain until Jesus comes. So too with sickness and suffering; they will be around until Jesus comes. God can heal and sometimes does heal. But not because it is His secret will that everybody be healed. We all have to die sometime. I think it is quite right to pray for people's healing and to do so with the Lord's Prayer in mind, as long as you submit to the possibility that He may choose not to heal. Then is the time to say, "The will of the Lord be done." It shows that you dignify His will.

The basic meaning of this third petition, "Your will be done," is that we plead with God to have His way on earth, as revealed in Scripture. That righteousness will prevail. That the church will flourish. That the gospel will succeed. We keep praying—on and on and on—whether or not we see our prayers answered. Why keep praying? Because we are commanded to do so.

It is a prayer we must mean with all our hearts. As John Stott said, it is folly to resist God's will. It is wisdom to discern it, to desire it, and to do it. Our prayer therefore is that God will get what He wants in *us*, at least. I cannot speak for anybody else. I am responsible to mean it when I say, "Lord, in *me*, Your will be done as You have wanted it accomplished in heaven." I pray that what God envisages for me will be carried out without a whimper or a whine, but only with complete submission. It means dignifying His will. That is what God is after.

PART 3

GOD'S PRAYER
LIST FOR US

CHAPTER 7

DAILY DEPENDENCE

Give us today our daily bread.
—MATTHEW 6:11

THIS IS THE fourth petition of the Lord's Prayer, the first on God's prayer list for us. The prayer changes from "your" to "us" and "our": "Give *us* this day *our* daily bread." This suggests we are part of a wider body of believers—a part of the family of God. We are all in this together. We think of ourselves, yes, but also of others who are praying this prayer.

God not only wants what is best for us by asking us to focus first on Him; He shows He cares about our daily struggles by focusing on our daily needs. We are now given the green light to give attention to ourselves when we pray.

But He sets the agenda! Yes, He now ordains that we pray for ourselves. But He knows what is best for us and in what order the needs should be mentioned. The remaining petitions pertain to what we need. God has promised to supply all our needs according to His riches in glory (Phil. 4:19). Jesus will say later on in the Sermon on the Mount, "So do not worry, saying, 'What shall we eat?' or 'What shall we drink?' or 'What shall we wear?'...Your heavenly Father knows that *you need them*" (Matt. 6:31–32, emphasis mine). So here we are invited to *pray* for our needs.

It may seem an incongruity: to pray for what God has already promised to supply anyway! But that is the way it is. He invites us to participate in His care for us. There are times when we wonder if God has forgotten. It is comforting to know that He knows this too; hence we pray daily for these essentials to life. The grandeur and glory of God now condescend to our own personal situation. I also think of John Wesley's principle, that God does nothing but in answer to prayer.

Imagine this! The great Creator and sovereign God of heaven and earth stoops to where we are. "For this is what the high and exalted One says—he who lives forever, whose name is holy: 'I live in a high and holy place, but also with the one who is contrite and lowly in spirit, to revive the spirit of the lowly and to revive the heart of the contrite'" (Isa. 57:15). The Most High God invites us to pray about the smallest of things. But don't worry about praying over small things; with God everything is small.

And yet to pray for daily bread is no small thing. When we live in a land of plenty, this may seem small. But when you live in a place where you don't know where your next meal is coming from, this request is far from small.

My dad lived through the Great Depression of 1929 and used to talk about it. He described how he once watched five hundred men stand in line for employment when there was only one job to be given out. The sight was so traumatic that my dad would weep as he recalled it. It is possible that we could one day enter another era like that of 1929. If so, the petition we now deal with—"Give us today our daily bread"—is very relevant indeed.

Physical Bread Is Our Lord's Priority for Us

Jesus begins with the undoubted priority: our daily bread.

But this surprises some. For this reason, many suppose that "daily bread" refers to spiritual bread, since Jesus called Himself the "bread of life" (John 6:35). Could this petition therefore refer to spiritual food? I reply: it might have referred to spiritual food and drink, but not in this case. You may think that God would put our spiritual needs first—as in praying for forgiveness, to be led away from temptation, and so forth.

But no. He Himself tells us what to pray for first. He begins with the *body*. The Lord's Prayer deals with the whole man: body, soul, spirit. God chose to give us bodies. God gave Jesus a body. "A body you prepared for me" (Heb. 10:5), our Lord envisaged, before the Word became flesh (John 1:14). God dignified our bodies by preparing a body for the second person of the Godhead when He came to the earth. So in this magnificent prayer, God begins the unfolding of His prayer list for us with a reference to our body. "For he knows how we are formed, he remembers that we are dust" (Ps. 103:14).

But why would God begin with the body and not the soul?

The truth is, it is extremely difficult to cope spiritually when we are unwell—hungry, thirsty, tired, deep in debt, going without sleep, and having no money. I think that is why Jesus put this request first, prior to spiritual needs. General William Booth, founder of the Salvation Army, used to say it is hard to preach the gospel to someone with an empty stomach. Likewise, it is hard to pray when we are overwhelmed with daily physical, emotional, and material problems.

I think also that Jesus begins with this particular petition to let us know that *God knows* our situation and remembers what we are like—"dust," as the psalmist put it. God knows we have to eat to live. God made this a priority.

I believe too that God put this petition here to remind us that there are starving people all over the world. When we sit down to eat, we should pray for those who have no food. I fear that most of us take for granted that we will eat today and tomorrow. It does not worry us. But it should at least make us grateful that we have bread on the table. This petition is designed therefore also to make us grateful and to pray for those in deep need.

Not only that, but when we pray, "Give *us* today *our* daily bread," we should be conscious of the entire body of Christ. If, for example, I have a pain in my toe or hand, I might say, "My toe hurts," or, "My hand hurts," but it is also right to say that "I hurt." In other words, my whole body feels the pain. Likewise, if there are those around us who suffer, we should feel their pain. And if there are those who are in fear of not having food for today, we should feel for those in the body— wherever they may be in the world—when we pray, "Give us today our daily bread." If there is one person suffering who is a part of the body of Christ, I should feel it—and should pray for anyone who is suffering at the present time. That is partly what is meant by this petition, "Give us today our daily bread"—not just *my* daily bread, but yours too.

The Lord's Prayer ought to make us aware of that multitude no one can count and make us feel what all believers are feeling. We are told to rejoice with those who rejoice and weep with those who weep (Rom. 12:15). Praying this particular petition, then, ought to serve to make us share in the sufferings of fellow believers in our immediate community yet also throughout the world. We are part of a vast body. It is huge. It includes all those who have been chosen from the foundation of the world. We must feel we are indeed our "brother's keeper" (Gen. 4:9). We should therefore think of others—those in need—when we pray, "Give us today our daily bread." It is a way—even if it is a small way—that we can intercede for those who do not have what we have. And it certainly ought to make us very grateful indeed that we are so blessed.

"Daily Bread" Means Essential Needs

"Daily bread" refers not only to food on our tables but to life's essential needs. This petition does not refer to literal bread only. "Bread" in Hebrew meant all kinds of nutrition. But it is even more than that. "Daily bread" refers to everything nonspiritual that we must have to live and cope. It refers to physical needs, emotional needs, material needs—every need not specifically mentioned in the petitions of the Lord's Prayer.

Therefore, when you pray, "Give us today our daily bread," you are asking God to step in to give you not only food but also shelter and clothing; to supply your financial needs; to give emotional strength and clarity of mind; to give you friends and fellowship; to grant transportation as needed; to equip you for your job, career, and future; to help you get done what you need to get done this very day; to be at your best; to help you in your preparation; and to provide providences that further God's plan for your life. "Our daily bread," then, covers everything that is essential to our well-being in life.

The psychologist Abraham Maslow (1908–1970) argued

that people everywhere are subject to what he called a "hier-archy of needs." At the bottom are things such as food, shelter, and sleep, these being elementary physiological needs. Next come the basic needs for safety and security. As you move up Maslow's pyramid you come to what he called "belonging needs" (love, acceptance, affiliation). Then come "esteem needs" (self-respect, social status, the approval of others). At the top of the pyramid is "self-actualization" (a musician must make music, an artist must paint, a poet must write if they are going to be at peace with themselves). It is not farfetched to apply this petition—"Give us today our daily bread"—to these kinds of needs. We all have these needs. Our Lord graciously leads us to pray for such. What a wonderful God we have!

What Maslow calls self-actualization is what I call one's anointing, or gifting. It is what you are born to do—and what comes easily. We all need to discover our gifts, our calling. Praying the Lord's Prayer therefore includes the petition that you will discover your own particular calling. If, then, you feel you have not yet discovered your calling— what your own anointing is—you have a perfect right to pray this petition with precisely that in mind!

This petition is also a reference to nature. Contrary to many of the church fathers, "our daily bread" is not a refer-ence to our spirituality. The church fathers missed this point entirely—including Tertullian, Cyprian, and Augustine, who said this request referred to spiritual food. They alle-gorized this petition, claiming that it referred to invisible bread, the Lord's Supper. "Absurd," said John Calvin, who normally affirmed the church fathers. The Reformers were down-to-earth in their treatment of this petition. Calvin said this petition refers to whatever God knows to be essential.

Martin Luther said it meant everything necessary for the preservation of this life: food, a healthy body, good weather, house, home, children, good government—even peace.

John Stott observed that to decline to mention our needs on the ground that we should not bother God with such trivialities is as great an error as to allow trivialities to dominate our prayers.

This petition is therefore a reference to essential nourishment of the whole man—body, spirit, soul, mind. There can be no doubt that this petition also reflects the Old Testament account of the daily manna that God provided supernaturally from heaven. The children of Israel were given manna every day—enough for everyone, and twice the amount on Friday so they would not have to go looking for manna on the Sabbath (Exod. 16:13–30). Although the manna itself was supernatural, the purpose was to keep the Israelites alive.

While some of us, sadly, live to eat, Jesus assumes we must eat in order to live. Furthermore, unless we are fasting on purpose, the assumption is that we must nourish our bodies every day; we should be thankful for food to eat every day. Keep in mind too that Jesus originally addressed an agrarian society. One crop failure spelled disaster. Not only that, but laborers were paid daily for the work they achieved. The pay was so low that it was almost impossible to save anything. The day's pay purchased the day's food.

This petition, then, was no empty rhetoric for Jesus' original hearers. Food nowadays, however, comes to countries like the United States and the United Kingdom from all over the world. When I grew up we got to eat strawberries only once a year. But now you can eat strawberries every day! This is true with most fruits and vegetables.

God Himself is the ultimate source of every good thing. "Every good and perfect gift is from above, coming down from the Father of the heavenly lights, who does not change like shifting shadows" (Jas. 1:17). This refers also to having a job. The prayer does not mean, "Do not work—just ask God to feed you," however. We are all under the curse of the fall. Like it or not, the decree in the Garden of Eden—"By the sweat of your brow you will eat your food until you return to the ground" (Gen. 3:19)—is still in play. Said Paul to his converts: "For even when we were with you, we gave you this rule: 'The one who is unwilling to work shall not eat'" (2 Thess. 3:10).

Thank God for your job; thank Him for income. But do not take the Lord's Prayer as a way of avoiding your responsibilities!

Sleep is a physical need. "He grants sleep to those he loves" (Ps. 127:2). There are times I feel the Lord does not love me—as when I can't sleep! I know what it is to fear not sleeping when I have to get up early in the morning. It is a neurotic problem I have had most of my life. When I do not have to get up early, I can usually sleep well. When I know I have to get up early to meet a schedule, I sometimes stay awake the whole night! I have learned to be thankful for every good night's sleep. When I have not slept well, I cannot think as clearly. I have difficulty reading my Bible and praying—not to mention writing. The Lord's Prayer therefore is a request to get the sleep we need. And I am very thankful indeed for a good night's sleep.

Your daily bread includes the ability to work. We should be thankful we can work, and we should keep in mind those who cannot because of disability or being bedridden. Thank God that you have a job; thank Him that you have an ability to do your job. Thank Him for strength, health, intelligence, peace. My own calling is teaching and preaching. I live for insight. If Abraham Maslow's concept of self-actualization is correct, I am at the peak of my anointing when I am seeing things in Scripture I had not read or thought of before. I pray all the time for insight. It is my daily bread, so to speak. We all need encouragement, approval, appreciation, and acceptance to perform at our best. When I receive insight, it makes me feel more accepted by my heavenly Father than anything! And yet when I also have the encouragement and acceptance of those around me, it spurs me on to work better.

This petition therefore refers to emotional needs. You need attention—to be noticed, to be recognized, to be affirmed. It is a natural need. Be thankful every day that such needs are met. Think of those who are suffering in this area at the moment. They are all around you. Pray, "Give us this day *our* daily bread," for those in the body of Christ who suffer emotional deprivation. And be thankful that your needs are being met. Be thankful every single day.

We can all do with a compliment now and then! I will never forget two letters I received the same day. The first I opened was regarding my book *The Anointing*. A man tore it to shreds, really putting the book down in his letter. I was quite devastated. Then I opened the second letter. It too, would you believe, was about my book *The Anointing*. The person wrote to thank me and tell me how much it encouraged them. It reminded me of a story about Uncle Buddy Robinson. Someone approached him after a sermon and said, "That is the best sermon I ever heard." Uncle Buddy prayed, "Lord, don't let me get puffed up." A second or two later, someone said to him about the same sermon, "That's the worst sermon I ever heard." Uncle Buddy prayed, "Lord, don't let me get puffed down."

This petition is a reference to *now*. "Give us *today* our daily bread." It is easier to pray about the distant future than to pray, "Give us today our daily bread." Most of us in the affluent West have enough for today and tomorrow, with food in freezers. Why should you and I pray for daily bread *today*? Because we must stay conscious of daily dependence, whether for strength, energy, sleep, health—all that will challenge us today.

This word *daily* comes from a Greek word that is found nowhere else except in Matthew 6:11 and Luke 11:3, the two references to the Lord's Prayer in the New Testament. It is a word not found in Hellenistic literature nor in the Septuagint (the Greek translation of the Old Testament). Most scholars believe that the Lord has coined a word. What does "daily" bread mean? Don Carson believes the best translation is "coming day." If prayed in the morning, it means *today*. If prayed in the evening, it means *tomorrow*.

But what about Matthew 6:34, "Do not worry about tomorrow, for tomorrow will worry about itself"? Michael Eaton, a prolific English writer and preacher, said praying about tomorrow is the means by which we are free from anxiety about tomorrow. If I pray the Lord's Prayer in the evening, I pray for the needs of the coming day, so I can go to sleep. After all, Paul said, "Do not be anxious about anything, but in every situation, by prayer and petition, with thanksgiving, present your requests to God" (Phil. 4:6).

The Purpose of This Petition

The purpose of the petition "Give us today our daily bread" is to warn us against greed. Why? Because it refers to what is *immediate*—"today" (or tomorrow, if prayed at night). Not next week or next month or next year. It pertains only to what you and I *need*. It is not a prayer to win the lottery. In economics there are essentially three levels: needs, comforts, luxuries. This prayer embraces only *needs*. Necessities. What I need to survive day by day. Most of us in the affluent West have more than enough.

I return to this matter of being thankful. The purpose of this petition is to teach us gratitude. God loves gratitude; He hates ingratitude. The psalmist learned gratitude. "Give thanks to the LORD, for he is good" (Ps. 106:1). "Give thanks to the LORD, for he is good" (Ps. 107:1). "Since we are receiving a kingdom that cannot be shaken, *let us be thankful*" (Heb. 12:28, emphasis mine). Learn to be thankful for the smallest thing. And then tell Him! When ten lepers were miraculously healed by Jesus, only one came back to Him to say, "Thank You." Jesus' immediate comment was, "Were not all ten cleansed? Where are the other nine?" (Luke 17:17). God notices when we are thankful and when we are not (or forget to tell Him).

We should also take the time to thank God for our food before we eat. This should be done when you are alone and when you are in public. Do not be ashamed to pray out loud if this is appropriate. And you don't need to bow your head and close your eyes as you give thanks, to be seen of people (that would be a wrong motive). But rather be unashamed and thankful to God. We should realize our debt to God every single day. God does not owe us these things. The irony of today's generation is that our wealth has made us more thankless than ever. It is an outrage, a disgrace. God have mercy on us! May we fill in the gap whenever we have a chance—to be thankful to God and tell Him so.

The further purpose of this petition is to show our daily dependence on God. We referred earlier to the manna. God provided every day, never in advance (except for the Sabbath), so there would be a daily sense of debt and dependence on our Father. The Israelites were totally dependent on God, one day at a time. They were in the desert, where there was no food. How would you like that kind of existence? And yet that is the way God wants us to trust Him. One of the most startling verses in the Old Testament is this: "The manna stopped the day after they ate this food from the land"—that is, after they entered the land of Canaan (Josh. 5:12).

Never, never, never take for granted all the good things God provides us. Where would we be without food, shelter, clothing, job, friends, emotional support, health, sleep, gifting to do our job? We are dependent every day.

A farmer in Kansas was worried about his wheat crop. There had not been rain in weeks. To keep his crops from being totally lost, he took buckets of water from his well and poured water on the crops. This meant hour after hour after hour of pouring water on the soil so he would not lose everything. But the well also began to go dry, until the farmer realized he had to stop using this water. He was seemingly at the end of hope. He merely said, "Lord, unless You send rain immediately, all I have is gone." The next day he saw clouds that began to form rain. The rain came and soaked the area thoroughly in just a few minutes. The farmer took a chair out to the wheat field and sat in the chair as the rain came down on his face.

His wife said, "Have you lost your mind?"

"No," he replied, "I am just enjoying seeing God do so easily what was so hard for me to do."

In 1962–1963, Louise and I lived in Ohio, where I was a pastor of a small church. We went through a very difficult time. The treasurer had to cut back on our salary, which was never adequate in the first place. We had no money in the bank. We wondered how we would make it through the day. That very day a gift came in the mail from someone we had not seen in years. An old friend wrote to say, "My wife woke up thinking of you and felt we should send you this check." This is something that only God could make happen.

God is never too late, never too early, but always just in time.

CHAPTER 8

A PLEA AND A DECLARATION

Forgive us our debts, as we also have forgiven our debtors.
—MATTHEW 6:12

I BELIEVE THE GREATEST need of the church today is to heed the petition now before us. I have prayed that this part of my book will make a definite difference in your own personal life. I don't want this chapter to give you any pseudo-guilt; neither do I want what follows to be threatening to you. But I do suspect there will be many who read this book who feel that this is the most important section of the Lord's Prayer. If so, our Lord Himself would agree with you, because at the close of the Lord's Prayer Jesus added a P.S., this being His only and immediate comment on what He just said: "For if you forgive other people when they sin against you, your heavenly Father will also forgive you. But if you do not forgive others their sins, your Father will not forgive your sins" (Matt. 6:14–15). Of all the petitions He gave in the Lord's Prayer, this is the only one He referred to.

This fifth petition of the Lord's Prayer is the first that deals with our spiritual needs. Many of us are familiar with the language "Forgive us our trespasses, as we forgive those who trespass against us." (William Tyndale used this rendering in his English New Testament, and it was adopted into the Anglican *Book of Common Prayer*.) The similar account in Luke 11:4 reads, "Forgive us our sins, for *we also forgive everyone who sins against us*" (emphasis mine).

My best-known sermon is probably the one called "Total Forgiveness." Wherever I preach it all over the world, the response is quite tremendous. I preached this once to five thousand people. I would estimate that forty-five hundred stood and came forward when I gave the appeal. Frequently, the overwhelming majority of all my congregations will respond by publicly admitting they have not forgiven but promise to do so at once. I sometimes believe I could preach the same exact sermon three weeks later and get a similar response from the same people. Why? Forgiving those who have been unjust, wicked, evil, and vile is the hardest thing in the world to do. Not only that, you have to *keep doing it*— days later, weeks later, years later. I know what I am talking about. I struggle in this area; I have to keep forgiving all the time. It is so easy to slip and repeat the same sin. This is why the Lord's Prayer needs to be prayed all the time.

I suppose this petition has made liars out of more people than any other document in human history! But don't blame Jesus for this. Just be sure you mean what you say when you make a plea—"Forgive us our trespasses"—and then make a declaration, or promise, in the same breath, "as we forgive those who have trespassed against us."

This petition is a plea for forgiveness: "Forgive us our sins." So far, so good. But the declaration is that we also have indeed forgiven those who have sinned against us. If *declaration* is too strong a word (stating that we *have* forgiven others), it is at least a promise that we *will* do so. If I feel convicted of an untruth as I pray this petition, I immediately want to promise God that from now on I will forgive those who have sinned against me.

However, my insertion of making a promise to God is my own idea. It is not what Jesus said. Taking Jesus' word literally, I am either telling the truth or I am not when I say to Him that *I have forgiven those* who have trespassed against me. But if, when I pray this petition, I fear that I may not have forgiven those who have sinned against me, I should promise Him at once that I certainly *will* forgive them—and do so immediately.

Do we realize what we are saying when we pray this heart-searching petition? First we are asking God to forgive us our sins, our "debts." The Greek *opheilemata* means "that which is owed."[1] It is used interchangeably with *hamartias*—"falling short" or "sins,"[2] as in Luke 11:4 and Matthew 6:14–15. We owe a great debt to God: pure obedience. Anything that comes short of His glory is *sin*. This is why all have sinned and come short of the glory of God (Rom. 3:23). We are all sinners. There is no one who does not sin (2 Chron. 6:36). We owe God lives of transparent obedience. But we all fail.

We therefore ask God to let us off the hook. The Greek word *aphiemi* means to "let be" or "send away."[3] So we pray that God will overlook our debt. Instead of our having to pay, we pray He will leave it as it is—that He will let it be without holding us responsible. We simply ask God to wipe away our debt.

Aren't you glad that Jesus gave us this petition? God knows our frame and remembers that we are dust (Ps. 103:14). The same God who requires us to be holy (Lev. 11:44; 1 Pet. 1:16) simultaneously gives the green light to pray for forgiveness because He knows we will fall. This is so wonderful. He is so gracious and understanding.

I was brought up in a church that taught not only that we must not sin but that we can indeed live above sin. The impact of this teaching went so deep that I still feel the effects of it to this day. I will not attempt to explain their rationale for how we could live without ever sinning, only to say that I wondered in those days why we have the Lord's Prayer if indeed it is possible to live without sin. Why would Jesus even give us this prayer if there were a possibility that Christians could live without ever sinning?

The Lord's Prayer sets us free from the sinless perfectionist syndrome of those who fancy they can live without sin. Some manage this kind of sanctification (1) by refusing to call some sins *sin* by substituting the word *mistake, error,* or *shortcoming* so they can claim to have lived without "sin"; or (2) because they see sin only as external—for example, the physical acts of murder or adultery (not apparently realizing that Jesus regarded hate and lust as sin). The point is Jesus knew we would sin and need to pray this prayer He gave us, which He worded perfectly for our benefit.

But as we have seen, the Lord's Prayer goes a step further. We might wish Jesus had not added this. But with the plea for forgiveness, He adds a declaration we make when we pray—that we have already forgiven others as God has forgiven us. Oh dear. What a declaration! We claim that we have forgiven others as God has forgiven us. We are put on the spot to forgive everyone—or forfeit praying the prayer altogether.

Why would Jesus put the petition this way? Such wording brings His teaching home to us in a very personal way. You might feel this is unfair. If so, you would not have liked His teaching in the Sermon on the Mount, as when He said, "Love your enemies and pray for those who persecute you" (Matt. 5:44). If, then, we are going to be followers of Jesus, we do get a wonderful fringe benefit—to be able to pray the Lord's Prayer—but we are trapped! We have to promise to forgive. We cannot pick and choose which of these petitions suits us. We are brought face to face with the heart of Jesus' teaching on the kingdom of heaven and are forced to apply His words—or not pray this prayer at all.

So this petition is a plea and virtually a promise: a plea for forgiveness and a declaration that we have forgiven. And I would hope that if we pray the prayer, and realize we have *lied* when we profess to have forgiven those who sinned against us, we would turn that declaration into a promise to forgive—at once.

What the Prayer for Forgiveness Is Not

The plea "Forgive us our trespasses" is not a prayer for salvation. It is not a prayer to be saved, born again, or justified before God. It is not a "sinner's prayer," as in the parable of the two men in the temple. The publican prayed, "God, have mercy on me, a sinner" (Luke 18:13). But this petition is not that at all.

The proof that this petition is not a prayer for salvation is that we are saved by faith—plus nothing! "For it is by grace you have been saved, through faith—and this is not from yourselves, it is the gift of God—not by works, so that no one can boast" (Eph. 2:8–9). If we pleaded for forgiveness on the basis of what we have done ("as we forgive those who trespass against us"[4]), salvation would be conditional. It would mean we are saved on the condition that we have forgiven already, as if this qualifies us to be saved. That would also mean salvation by works. *Forgiving others is a work*—and a very noble work indeed. We could never claim we are saved by the sheer grace of God if our salvation depended upon forgiving others. If that were the case, who would be saved?

Nobody could be saved if we had to forgive before we could be justified. Forgiving others is a grace of the Holy Spirit. When you bless your enemies, you have crossed over into the supernatural. You could only do this by the Holy Spirit, and you do not have the Holy Spirit until you have been converted. Therefore you—and no one else—would be required to forgive those who have sinned against you *before* you could be a part of the family of God. And even if you take the view that you promise to forgive if you realize you haven't, this too is not a condition for being saved; it would mean that you are saved by works. It would also imply you are kept by works. Wrong. We are saved by grace and kept saved by grace. In a word: we are not saved by forgiving others; we are not kept saved by forgiving others.

Why, then, this petition? It is a necessary prayer for a child of God who has already been saved to *enjoy fellowship with the Father* and also to *inherit fully His kingdom*. "But," someone will ask, "is not salvation the same as forgiveness of our sins? And is not this what we are commanded to pray for?" Yes. But it is also the kind of prayer every Christian continues to pray. We are brought to salvation by praying for the forgiveness of all our sins, yes; but we continue to pray this way after we are saved. The wonderful verse "If we confess our sins, he is faithful and just and will forgive us our sins and purify us from all unrighteousness" (1 John 1:9) is actually a prayer for the *Christian* to pray, although it has been used countless times to lead a person to Christ.

John also said, "If we claim to be without sin, we deceive ourselves and the truth is not in us" (1 John 1:8), a verse that flies in the face of sinless perfection teaching. "Who can say, 'I have kept my heart pure; I am clean and without sin'?" (Prov. 20:9). "There is no one on earth...who does what is right and never sins" (Eccles. 7:20). The closer we are to God, the more aware we are of our sin; and the more we inherit the kingdom and enjoy fellowship with the Father, the greater will we feel the need to pray the Lord's Prayer. (See Isaiah 6:1–5, where the prophet Isaiah feels convicted of sin when he sees the glory of God.)

What the Prayer for Forgiveness Is

The Lord's Prayer is a believer's prayer. First, we pray "Our Father," which, as we saw earlier, presupposes we are in the family of God. Second, the petition "hallowed be your name" would only be uttered by a converted man or woman. Third, to pray "your kingdom come" is to be uttered by one already in the kingdom who is wanting to inherit all that God has for him or her. All Christians have the Holy Spirit, and yet Paul urged us to "be filled with the Spirit" (Eph. 5:18). That is arguably the main point of the Lord's Prayer. Fourth, praying for the forgiveness of sins is not a green light to sin on and on but a consciousness that we have fallen short. We want to keep short accounts with God and confess our sins immediately to enjoy His presence and fellowship.

A further purpose of this petition, then, is not only to enjoy fellowship with the Father in ever-increasing measure but also to keep us from a feeling of self-righteousness.

Self-righteousness is deadly. It is the easiest sin to commit and the hardest to see in ourselves. Only a profound grasp of Scripture and a great sense of God's holy presence will keep one alerted to their sinfulness; otherwise, self-righteousness creeps in painlessly like a cancer and will be our downfall if not detected. Strange as it may seem, Christians who grievously fall are often the most self-righteous, before and after their sin. Only the Holy Spirit will make us aware of our sin.

The truth is we need the daily forgiveness of our sins as much as we do our daily bread. Keep in mind that this is the first spiritual petition in the Lord's Prayer. It is a prayer to be cleansed. As Calvin put it, our sins are like a dividing wall that prevents God from coming close, and like a cloud that stops His eyes from seeing us. "You have covered yourself with a cloud so that no prayer can get through" (Lam. 3:44).

Therefore, when we want to get close to God, we start *not* by telling Him how faithful we have been, or how righteous we are, but by praying for the remission of our sins. This way we are sure our prayers reach God. This is why when we come boldly to the throne of grace, our first request is to ask for mercy to find grace to help us in our time of need (Heb. 4:16). Mercy is what we ask for in the sinner's prayer, as we saw earlier. It is what we ask for first when we approach the throne of grace. Let no one think that he or she ever—*ever*—outgrows the need for mercy!

Basic Assumptions

There are two assumptions in this petition—first, that we need to be forgiven. Let us not take this for granted. Jesus knows we will need to be forgiven. Let me say emphatically that He is not talking about sin with a high hand, as in deliberately breaking the sixth or seventh commandment. Not that committing murder or adultery cannot be forgiven (it can; see Psalm 51, the prayer of David after his adultery and murder). Some Christians have fallen grievously and bring shame upon God's name. Jesus is not talking about sin that we intend to commit as soon as we get the chance; that would be mockery. The prayer of 1 John 1:9 means that you are truly sorry. Praying the petition "Forgive us our debts" is a prayer of contrition, that you are truly sorry for your debts, trespasses, sins, failures.

The first assumption, then, is that we are not perfect. Jesus wants us to be aware of the fact that we have come short of His glory—and do so all the time. Anyone with a degree of conscientiousness and awareness of God's holiness knows this. This is why we pray: because we are weak.

The second assumption is that people have hurt us. We know that we ourselves have come short of God's glory. Other people too have come short of God's glory and have hurt us. Have you ever considered the possibility that when an acquaintance of yours prays this petition, it is actually *you they are having to forgive*? Does this surprise you? We have all been hurt. We have all hurt others. The cliché "hurt people hurt people" is so true. We all have failed.

We all have a story to tell about how hurt we have been. Some have been hurt more than others. I know what it is to be hurt, but when I hear of another's suffering, I blush that I could have even thought of being hurt. Some of you reading these lines have been sinned against terribly. There are those who have been raped. Abused as a child. Lied about. Walked over by an authority figure. Had an unfaithful spouse. Were let down by a Christian leader.

Or let us say it is a "lesser evil." Someone hurt your feelings. You did not get invited to a party. Someone did not speak to you as they passed you (maybe they didn't see you!). You did not get the credit when you did a good deed. You thought someone would be nicer than they were. You thought they would say yes to your request, but they turned you down.

Sometimes we have to forgive a person who did no wrong at all. I had to forgive a famous theologian for not recommending one of my books when I thought he should. He did no wrong, but I had to forgive him! (I didn't tell him, of course; it happened in my heart.) By the way, don't walk up to someone and say, "I forgive you." They will ask, "For what?" And you will incur a greater misunderstanding and tension than ever. The *only* time you say, "I forgive you," is when another is asking for forgiveness. The real reason we usually say, "I forgive you," without someone asking for it is because we want to be sure they know how hurt we are! Saying you forgive them will always backfire and be counterproductive.

It is a sobering fact that most of the people we have to forgive don't even think they have done anything wrong. I can safely guarantee that if I told you of my deepest hurts and won you over to my point of view, and you went to my offender, they would say with a straight face they did nothing wrong at all. They would pass a lie detector test with flying colors! It is absolutely true that most people who have hurt us don't think we should be hurt at all. But we feel the same way toward those who are having to forgive us. I believe there are many people who have had to forgive me. For exactly what I do not know, but I am sure their hurt is utterly real to them.

The truth is we have all sinned, and we have all been sinned against. Jesus gives us this petition that we might be forgiven of our own sin and failure—and that we in turn will show our gratitude for being forgiven by forgiving *everyone* who has hurt us.

Jesus shows that He knows what we know: *we have been hurt*. It is so kind of Him. We may have been discredited, dishonored, disappointed. We are therefore hurt. We have been lied about, taken advantage of, unappreciated. Some have been disloyal to us.

Thus, two assumptions lie behind this petition: we need to be forgiven, and we need to forgive.

However, this petition is an admission that we need forgiveness. Don't pray the Lord's Prayer if you feel no need of forgiveness or feel that you are so perfect in yourself. This petition is an implicit admission: "It is forgiveness I need."

But again, it is an admission—a declaration—that you have already forgiven those who have sinned against you. Have you? Have you forgiven those who have hurt you, let you down, disappointed you? Have you? You need to decide whether you will stop praying the Lord's Prayer or truly let others off the hook as God has let you off the hook. You must decide whether to pray this petition and pray for their not having the book thrown at them, as you want God not to throw the book at you. Or do you want God to throw the book at you? Are you prepared to say that you have done nothing wrong—that you are willing for all that is knowable about you, your thoughts and deeds, to be laid bare before all who know you?

This Petition Is a Covenant

This petition is actually an agreement, indeed a covenant with God. A covenant is a contract between two parties. In this petition you put yourself under a covenant with God— and implicitly with those who have sinned against you, even though the party who has offended you will have no idea you are making this agreement. The agreement is this: you agree to forgive them as you pray for your own forgiveness. Implied in this covenant is that you agree to be forgiven *in proportion* to the way you forgive. Yes. How does that make you feel? You agree for God to forgive *you* in proportion to the way you have let *others* off the hook. In other words, the degree to which you have let others off the hook will be the degree to which you ask God to let you off the hook. Are you OK with this? I can tell you, that is what this petition really means.

Some take the view that you don't have to forgive them unless they are sorry. Really? Where did you get that? I suspect that people adopt this view to keep from having to let people off the hook. Caution: if you wait until they are sorry, I predict you will go to your grave in bitterness. This is the devil keeping you from being like Jesus. Who was sorry at the cross of Jesus? Who was repenting that they hammered in the nails? Instead of waiting for them to be sorry, Jesus prayed, "Father, forgive them, for they do not know what they are doing" (Luke 23:34). It may get our goat that they don't know what they have done to us. But they did not know what they did to Jesus, and He forgave them.

There are no conditions accompanying the Lord's Prayer that give even a loophole not to forgive until the other person is sorry. We don't have that luxury. It takes minimal grace to forgive when another is sorry; it takes maximum grace to forgive when they are not sorry or don't know what they have done. This petition is an invitation to explore maximum grace! To cross over into the supernatural—to do what defies a natural explanation!

Paul asked the Ephesians to forgive each other "just as in Christ God forgave you" (Eph. 4:32). When you pray this petition in the Lord's Prayer, you are declaring yourself to forgive others as you ask for your own forgiveness. You are implicitly agreeing to this, that you yourself will be forgiven by God in the same measure as you have forgiven others.

In a word: to be forgiven, you agree to forgive; if you don't forgive, you forfeit your own forgiveness. This is the covenant implicit in this prayer. As New Testament scholar Don Carson put it, there is no forgiveness to the one who does not forgive. But thankfully, this is not a prayer for justification before God. Thank God, it is not a prayer for salvation. It is a prayer for continued fellowship with God. "If we walk in the light, as he is in the light, we have fellowship with one another [that is, primarily with the Father, secondarily with each other], and the blood of Jesus, his Son, purifies us from all sin" (1 John 1:7).

Do you like the Lord's Prayer? Perhaps you need to decide whether to stop praying it or to mean it from the heart. I urge you to pray it; I plead with you to pray it. Paul said that a further reason for forgiveness is to keep us from being outsmarted by Satan (2 Cor. 2:11, NLT). When you hold a grudge, you beckon Satan to walk right in. Don't do that; don't give him that pleasure. Not only that, but holding a grudge can be damaging to your health. It can lead to arthritis, high blood pressure, heart disease, and kidney disease. Not forgiving can also damage you emotionally and cripple you with guilt. Total forgiveness is what will lead you to discover what you have been born to do. You will find your true anointing; you will enjoy self-actualization.

Total forgiveness means you get freedom in return. Great liberty indeed—a sense of God you may have lost years ago. Do you want that great nearness of God back again? Set others free. Let them off the hook. Ask God to bless them. What is more, you will be praying the Lord's Prayer from your heart.

CHAPTER 9

THE UNNECESSARY
PITFALL

And lead us not into temptation.
—MATTHEW 6:13

WE NOW DEAL with the sixth petition, which says, "And lead us not into temptation, but deliver us from the evil one" (Matt. 6:13). Some say we have two petitions here. In any case, I choose to deal with them one at a time.

The petition "Give us today our daily bread" (v. 11) deals with our physical, natural needs. But when Jesus introduced forgiveness, He brought in the spiritual dimension. This petition, "And lead us not into temptation," continues with our spiritual state. If we meant what we said when we prayed, "And forgive us our debts, as we also have forgiven our debtors" (v. 12), a wonderful fellowship with the Father is in existence. It means the Holy Spirit in us is ungrieved.

But there is more than one way to grieve the Holy Spirit. When Paul said, "And do not *grieve* the Holy Spirit of God, with whom you were sealed for the day of redemption" (Eph. 4:30, emphasis mine), he used a Greek word that means to get one's feelings hurt. We hurt the Holy Spirit's feelings chiefly by bitterness. This is why Paul followed this admonition with, "Get rid of all bitterness, rage and anger, brawling and slander, along with every form of malice. Be kind and compassionate to one another, forgiving each other, just as in Christ God forgave you" (Eph. 4:31–32). When we grieve the Holy Spirit, He does not desert us, but we do lose an anointing of peace, clear thinking, and a sense of His presence and fellowship.

Whereas bitterness and unforgiveness grieve the Spirit, so does succumbing to sexual temptation. Paul continues in Ephesians 5:3: "But among you there must not be even a hint of sexual immorality, or of any kind of impurity, or of greed, because these are improper for God's holy people." Therefore, the spiritual dimension of the Lord's Prayer embraces three areas: (1) forgiving one another by keeping a sweet spirit with no bitterness, (2) living a holy life and not falling into shame and unbelief, and (3) being spared of Satan succeeding with us, which I deal with in the next chapter.

The Most Difficult of the Petitions

The petition we now unpack is the most difficult to understand: "Lead us not into temptation" (Matt. 6:13). Many volumes have been written on this petition. New Testament scholar C. F. D. Moule has even written a probing monograph, "An Unsolved Problem in the Temptation-Clause in the Lord's Prayer."[1] So can I get to the meaning of this petition in one chapter?

We are dealing with the mystery of an unusual petition. This mystery turns generally on two matters: (1) the translation of the Greek *peirasmon*,[2] which means either temptation, testing, or trial, or all three; and (2) the strange request that *God* should not lead us into temptation or trial, which implies He may well so lead us. This is strange considering also this verse: "When tempted, no one should say, 'God is tempting me.' For God cannot be tempted by evil, nor does he tempt anyone; but each person is tempted when they are dragged away by their own evil desire and enticed" (Jas. 1:13–14). So if God cannot tempt us, is not Jesus implying otherwise in this petition?

But if *peirasmon* means "testing" or "trial," James also said, "Consider it pure joy, my brothers and sisters, whenever you face trials of many kinds, because you know that the testing of your faith develops perseverance" (Jas. 1:2–3). This verse sounds like it is a good thing when you face trials of many kinds! If this is "pure joy," why pray to avoid it? As theologian John Stott said, if trials are beneficial, why should we pray not to get led into them?

Before the New Testament came along, the Greek word *peirasmon* rarely ever meant temptation in the sense of enticement to sin, as in temptation to sexual sin. Basically, it meant "testing." But James clearly takes this word partly to refer to lust. *Peirasmon* is thus used two ways by James: (1) signifying testing or trial (James 1:2 and also James 1:12: "Blessed is the one who perseveres under trial because, having stood the test, that person will receive the crown of life that the Lord has promised to those who love him"); and (2) signifying lust, almost certainly sexual lust (James 1:13: "When tempted, no one should say, 'God is tempting me'"). Only the context helps us know the exact meaning. First Corinthians 10:13, possibly the first verse a new Christian should memorize, can be taken either way too: "No temptation has overtaken you except what is common to mankind.

And God is faithful; he will not let you be tempted beyond what you can bear. But when you are tempted, he will also provide a way out so that you can endure it."

The problem is further complicated by two more verses: "Things that cause people to stumble are bound to come, but woe to anyone through whom they come" (Luke 17:1); and "I have told you these things, so that in me you may have peace. In this world you will have trouble. But take heart! I have overcome the world" (John 16:33). This means that testing and temptation will always be around; they are unavoidable. Why, then, would Jesus have us pray, "Lead us not into temptation"? The implication is that God could keep us away from temptation or bring us out of temptation, trial, or testing.

The buck stops with the Father. He has the power to keep us from a condition conducive to testing. Jesus said, "Watch and pray so that you will not fall into temptation. The spirit is willing, but the flesh is weak" (Matt. 26:41). But in the Lord's Prayer we are told to ask that the Father will not lead us, which, as I said, implies He might do so. That, then, is where we begin: we are dealing with the mystery of an unusual petition. How do we make sense of it?

This petition points to the misery of what may be an unnecessary pitfall. A pitfall is unsuspected danger or difficulty. We must keep Luke 17:1 and John 16:33 in mind, along with these verses: "There is something else meaningless that occurs on earth: the righteous who get what the wicked deserve, and the wicked who get what the righteous deserve" (Eccles. 8:14); and "I have seen something else under the sun: The race is not to the swift or the battle to the strong, nor does food come to the wise or wealth to the brilliant or favor to the learned; but time and chance happen to them all" (Eccles. 9:11).

The Father's Heart

The heart of the Father is revealed in the Lord's Prayer. And this petition shows that He does not want us to suffer. He also knows the pain we will feel if we fall into sin. This is the essential reason for this petition. Our heavenly Father does not want us to suffer as a result of falling into sexual sin or unbelief. Falling into sexual sin brings pain sooner or later; falling into unbelief leads to grumbling, which grieves the Holy Spirit. Our Father is looking out for us in this petition.

It is a wicked world we live in. The Father knows this; Jesus knows this. Our gracious God wants His own people to avoid the misery of a needless pitfall. Therefore He shares with His family what is on His heart, namely, that we might avoid temptation. You don't sin without temptation preceding it. The best way to avoid sin is to avoid temptation. That is, I believe, our Lord's rationale in giving us this petition.

Temptation and Testing

There is an essential difference between temptation and testing. Temptation is what God *allows* to test us, and yet it comes immediately from *within*. We read that "God tested Abraham" (Gen. 22:1). It was a major test to see whether Abraham would obey when God put to him what appeared to be an unreasonable proposition: to offer his son Isaac. Sometimes God leads us in a manner that makes no sense at the time. This is the essence of testing. And yet we also read that "Jesus was led by the Spirit into the wilderness *to be tempted by the devil*" (Matt. 4:1, emphasis mine). This temptation was a testing. It was necessary that Jesus should become like us in every way, and part of this was to be made "perfect through what he suffered" (Heb. 2:10). This was so He, having learned what temptation is, would be "able to help those who are being tempted" (Heb. 2:18). In other words, there was a good reason the Spirit would lead Jesus into the wilderness to be tempted by Satan.

It is a reminder that there is a good reason for every way God leads us, including what He allows to happen. It is all for a purpose. It turns out that Abraham was ready for his testing; he came through with flying colors. He fully intended to offer Isaac but at the last moment was prevented. An angel stepped in and stopped Abraham. And God said, "Now I know that you fear God, because you have not withheld from me your son, your only son" (Gen. 22:12). The result was that God swore an oath to Abraham—arguably the highest privilege God ever bestows on His children here on earth (Gen. 22:16–17; Heb. 6:13).

Jesus too was ready for His testing. He resisted every overture Satan made to Him. After overcoming Satan in the desert, the "devil left him, and angels came and attended him" (Matt. 4:11). Mind you, this was not the first nor the last time Jesus would be tested. The whole of His life was one of continual pleasing the Father and resisting the devil. The desert experience was no doubt one of the most difficult ordeals for Him. But He had to resist temptation and fulfill the Law throughout His entire lifetime, all the way to the cross. When He uttered, "It is finished" (John 19:30), it not only meant that our debt to God was *paid in full* but that Jesus' ordeal of testing was over. After His life was over, having sat down at the right hand of God (Heb. 12:2), it could be said that Jesus was tempted at all points as you and I are, "yet he did not sin" (Heb. 4:15). Had Jesus sinned— even once—He would have been disqualified to be our Savior. But He passed the test, and having been "made perfect, he became the source of eternal salvation for all who obey him" (Heb. 5:9).

Temptation, particularly sexual temptation, comes from within (as we saw from James 1:13). We cannot blame God for our temptation. Temptation does not come from God but from inside ourselves. We are responsible for our own temptation. Indeed, temptation is our own responsibility. The immediate thought we often have when we are tempted is to imagine that it is a "setup" from God—that God is behind it and will overlook it if we give in. It is true that God allowed it, but it is not true that He is responsible for it. When God allows sexual temptation, it is a test to see whether we will pass or fail.

Joseph, son of Jacob, could not have known he was being earmarked as a future prime minister of Egypt. When he worked for Potiphar, an Egyptian officer, he faced sexual temptation. Potiphar's wife was attracted to Joseph and pleaded with him day after day, "Come to bed with me!" Joseph refused (Gen. 39:7–8). He may have felt nothing but pointlessness in refusing her. Still, the angels said, "Yes!" Joseph passed the test with flying colors.

All of us must pass the test of sexual temptation. If we fail, God may give us a second chance. Billy Graham said that it seems the devil gets 75 percent of God's best servants through sexual sin. Sexual temptation is natural and normal; it is not a sin to be tempted. We are all tempted. Jesus was tempted. It is sin when we give in to temptation.

It is therefore true that God may test us by allowing us to be tempted. If you ask me, "To what extent is it God's purposeful will to cause something to happen? And to what extent does He merely allow things to happen?" I reply: I don't know. Nobody does. We all, like Moses, want to get close to the burning bush to see why it doesn't burn up, but God says to all of us: "Stay back, and worship." (See Exodus 3:5). Don't try to figure everything out. It is impossible in this life to know the difference between what God purposes and what He allows. He wants us to worship Him and affirm Him without knowing everything first. If we knew all the answers we would no longer need faith. But when we don't know the answer yet trust Him nonetheless, that is true faith—and it pleases God (Heb. 11:1, 6).

The Importance of the Word *Into*

If testing is for our good—if overcoming temptation is a necessary victory in our development—why would Jesus have us pray, "Lead us not into temptation"? We are to pray that we shall not be brought *into* temptation. Michael Eaton reckons that the prayer makes sense if we emphasize the word *into*. We are not praying that we shall not be *tempted*; we know that we will be tempted sooner or later. We are not praying that we shall not be *tested*; we know that we will be tested sooner or later. We are praying that we shall not be *prematurely tested* by being brought into something beyond our strength. We pray that nothing will bring us into temptation and testing prematurely and unnecessarily.

Dr. Martyn Lloyd-Jones used to say to me that the worst thing that can happen to someone is to succeed before they are ready. This is because success often goes to one's head, and we are better off to have success delayed until we are mature. In much the same way, we pray that we will not be thrown into the deep end of testing until we are ready for it. This is what Michael Eaton means, and I believe this is a brilliant insight. We should pray that God will spare us of testing that we are not ready for, because we would possibly fail the test if such testing came too soon. Even Jesus' temptation in the desert came at the age of thirty, and He was the Son of God! This is surely the basic meaning of this petition.

There is such a thing as an unnecessary pitfall. We have all seen people who succeed before they are ready. And I have also seen people fall at an early age. I think of teenagers who face temptations far fiercer and greater than when I was a teenager. What is out there in the world at the present time is unimaginable evil and wickedness. The Lord's Prayer needs to be reintroduced to churches and Christians everywhere and prayed with utter earnestness. I commend churches that pray the Lord's Prayer regularly. And I believe the churches that never think of praying it do their members no favor by neglecting this extraordinary prayer.

King Saul is an example of a man who succeeded before he was ready. The temptation to pride seemed to have overcome him. He took himself too seriously, fancied that he could offer the burnt offerings even though he was not called to do this (1 Sam. 13:9). He became yesterday's man in the prime of his life.

Our prayer to God therefore is that He will not let us fall into a situation greater than we can cope with—that is, sooner than we are able to cope with it. The truth is we never know how strong we will be. I remember a conversation I had with theologian and philosopher Francis Schaeffer years ago, when I contemplated a certain academic course. He cautioned me that intellectual temptation is like sexual temptation; we never know how strong we will be. We must admit to our weakness. God knows what it is. We are therefore to be on bended knee that our Father will not allow us to be in an unnecessary situation.

You may ask, "What about 1 Corinthians 10:13?" This is the verse I believe every new Christian should memorize as soon as possible: "No temptation [in Greek, *peirasmon*— testing, trial, temptation] has overtaken you except what is common to man. And God is faithful; he will not let you be tempted beyond what you can bear. But when you are tempted, he will also provide a way out so that you can endure it." You may understandably argue that God will honor this word, regardless of whether a person is being tested prematurely.

True. We are all responsible, and God has made it clear that if we succumb to temptation, or fail in the testing, we are going against grace that was promised to us. But I would hope that my grandson—Tobias Robert Stephen Kendall, born during the writing of this book—would be spared a heavy testing and trial for a long, long time. It is any father's or grandfather's concern. And likewise it is our heavenly Father's concern for us. He is telling us to pray to be spared of falling *into* temptation, trial, or testing. My heart would ache to see my loved ones going through severe testing. I would not want it for them; you would not want it for your children and grandchildren. That is God's fatherly love for each of us too.

Two Possible Attitudes When
Praying This Petition

There are two ways you can pray this petition, "Lead us not into temptation." The first is, quite foolishly, to challenge God by demanding that He do it all for us—demanding He give us grace so that we won't feel so tempted. Take, for example, a person who is willing to fall. It may be that potential temptation is at hand. Perhaps they know they will meet someone this very day who will provide a very luring temptation. They know they should not give in. They also know they should avoid the temptation. But they say, "OK, God, give me grace today not to give in. If I give in, it's because You did not give me sufficient grace." That is blaming God. It is also what Jesus called tempting God. When Satan told Jesus to jump off the pinnacle of the temple, since it was promised that the angels would deliver Him and keep Him from hurting Himself, Jesus replied, "It is also written: 'Do not put the Lord your God to the test'" (Matt. 4:7).

When I willfully walk into a situation I know beforehand will mean fierce temptation, and I put the onus on God to uphold me, I am tempting Him. Therefore, to pray the petition, "Lead us not into temptation," when I am challenging God by walking deliberately into temptation, I am mocking Him. If I say, "But I prayed the Lord's Prayer, and the temptation still came," I am shifting the blame from myself to God. It is what the flesh will always try to do. This is precisely why James said, "When tempted, no one should say, 'God is tempting me.' For God cannot be tempted by evil, nor does he tempt anyone; but each person is tempted when they are dragged away by their own evil desire and enticed. Then, after desire has conceived, it gives birth to sin; and sin, when it is full-grown, gives birth to death. Don't be deceived, my dear brothers and sisters" (Jas. 1:13–16).

But there is a second way to pray this petition, "Lead us not into temptation." It is to pray with the fear that God may well allow one to fall. This is scary. When you pray, "Lead us not into temptation," being so mindful of your own weakness, as well as the possibility that God thinks you are equal to it, you are very sobered indeed. You therefore plead this petition on bended knee, as if to say, "O God, please help me, please, please do not let me come *into* temptation."

This second way of praying is the right spirit. It honors God. It takes into account that you know how weak you are. You know how easily you could fall. You don't want to fall, you don't want to displease God, you don't want to grieve the Spirit. So when you utter this plea, "Lead us not into temptation," you do so with gravity and earnestness and pray that God will indeed answer your prayer and *not let you enter into temptation*. This second way of praying is a heart cry to the Father, and this is the way Jesus means for us to pray this petition.

Question: How do *you*, dear reader, pray this petition?

The proof that you mean this prayer is that you will do all you can in your own power to avoid a temptation situation. You may recall that Jesus said in the Garden of Gethsemane, "Watch and pray so that you will not fall into temptation. The spirit is willing, but the flesh is weak" (Matt. 26:41). Note the order: "Watch and pray." He did not say, "Pray and watch." When you watch before you pray, you are already looking out for the danger. If you pray before you watch, you might want to shift the blame to God. "I prayed about it," you may say, "but the temptation still came. So God certainly let it happen." This is the devil talking. Jesus wisely asked the disciples to "watch and pray," which shows that you are assuming certain mature responsibilities as you pray. This is what pleases God.

Paul said, "Clothe yourselves with the Lord Jesus Christ, and do not think about how to gratify the desires of the flesh" (Rom. 13:14). Hearing St. Ambrose preach on this text led to St. Augustine's conversion. Augustine was a man who led a profligate lifestyle. The best way to avoid falling into sin is to avoid the temptation you know is out there. Evangelist Billy Sunday used to say that the reason so many Christians fall into sin is that they treat temptation like strawberry shortcake rather than a rattlesnake!

You prove how strong you are *not* by how you cope when being tempted but by seeing how far you can get from temptation.

Remember also that falling into sin can happen to anybody. This is why Paul cautioned us, "Brothers and sisters, if someone is caught in a sin, you who live by the Spirit should restore that person gently. But watch yourself, or you also may be tempted" (Gal. 6:1). Never approach the fallen Christian with a "pointing the finger" attitude. This will be counterproductive in your efforts; your self-righteousness will disqualify you from being a blessing. You can count on being rejected. Always go to the person who has fallen with this attitude: "This could have happened to me as easily as it happened to you. I am not better than you. It could be me next time but for the grace of God." The fallen person will more likely listen to you and get the help you have to offer when you approach him or her in that spirit.

The temptation, or testing, will mainly come in the form of (1) sexual temptation and (2) unbelief. The two can even come together simultaneously. You may find yourself asking, "Why did God let this happen to me? How could this happen, since I have prayed for it not to happen?" This is where unbelief will try to set in.

One of the main purposes of testing is to increase our faith. Testing has to come sooner or later. You pray it comes not one hour sooner than you are ready for it. But you may never feel you are ready. I think of some of the trials we had at Westminster Chapel. My twenty-five years in London were both the best and worst years of my life. I had the greatest trials I ever knew yet also the greatest thrills.

I thank God that Romanian evangelist Josef Tson reached me with his warning, "RT, you must totally forgive them," precisely when it came. The trial I was experiencing at that particular time was a picnic compared to what would come later. God graciously taught me to forgive—in the nick of time, I would say. It is what equipped me for greater testing. I am admitting that God was extraordinarily gracious to me. He did not let me be tested to the extreme until I was ready. What is more, my faith was increased. What I once thought was the worst thing that ever happened to me proved to be the best thing that ever happened to me. That's the truth!

Why Unanswered Prayer?

The mystery of this unusual petition is compounded by trying to grasp the meaning of unanswered prayer. The issue is this: What if, after you pray this petition, "Lead us not into temptation," from your heart—and after avoiding every possible pitfall—you still fall into a severe testing? I reply: God knows you are up to it. You are ready for it. Not only that, take it with both hands!

Here is why. When James says, "Consider it pure joy, my

brothers and sisters, whenever you face trials of many kinds" (Jas. 1:2), the Greek literally reads (in the KJV) to count it all joy when you "fall" into temptation. You fell into it. You didn't go out looking for it. It came to you; you passively fell into the trial. James did not say you fell morally; you merely fell into the trial. In a word: it came to you. The reason James says to consider it pure joy is because you can take that kind of trial as a gift from God.

The word *consider* in James 1:2 (NIV), or *count* (KJV), is the same exact word Paul uses in Romans 4:5, where it is translated "credited": "To the man who does not work but trusts God who justifies the wicked, his faith is *credited* as righteousness." We are justified by faith alone, not works. But we may not *feel* righteous. We take God's word for it; He credits us with righteousness. We are counted righteous as though we really were; and we *are* righteous—in His sight. We take His word for it that we are righteous. Feelings are one thing, faith another.

So too with James 1:2. We *count*, or *consider*, it pure joy when we fall into trials. We don't *feel* joy. Far from it; it may be the worst day of our life! But James said that we should count, or impute, to the trial pure joy. Why? Because if we knew the results of the trial, we would believe God's reason for counting it joy. As I said, the worst trial of my life became the best thing that ever happened to me. I must admit to you, sadly, that I did not consider it pure joy at the time. It was horrible. I should have, though. I did try to dignify that trial, and I even believe I did. But did I consider it "pure joy"? Probably not.

The point is this: we will later see what God has in mind for us when He allows us to "fall" into temptation, in His perfect timing. It is only a matter of time until we will see something of His rationale and strategy for letting it happen when it did.

So to answer the question "Why did God not answer our prayer when we prayed *not* to enter into temptation?" it means we were equal to the trial. God knew we could take it. He dignified us! We did not have to face it prematurely. We were ready for it. And we should pass the trial with flying colors! You were handed on a silver platter the means of sanctification: to refine your faith and character. "We also glory in our sufferings, because we know that suffering produces perseverance; perseverance, character; and character, hope" (Rom. 5:3–4).

I hope this helps to clarify the mystery of an unusual petition. We do indeed pray to avoid testing, even knowing that falling into trial is beneficial. We rejoice when persecuted (Matt. 5:11–12), but we don't go looking for it. God knows we will be equal to it if we wait for His timing. And when the sudden trial comes, *accept it as from His hand*. As the hymn puts it,

> Every joy or trial falleth from above,
> Traced upon our dial by the Sun of Love;
> We may trust him fully, all for us to do;
> They who trust Him wholly find Him wholly true.
> —FRANCES RIDLEY HAVERGAL (1836–79)[3]

Don't go looking for testing, but welcome it when it comes. Just realize that a sovereign God permitted it. The heart of the Father is that we will be happy and holy. This is why we have this petition. He wants us to be spared the misery of unnecessary pitfalls. But should He allow them after we have avoided them and prayed to avoid them, "Consider it pure joy" (Jas. 1:2).

You will eventually treasure the trial you are now in. Consider it pure joy—now.

CHAPTER 10

DAILY DELIVERANCE

But deliver us from the evil one.
—MATTHEW 6:13

THIS IS THE final petition in the Lord's Prayer. Whether it is part of the sixth or considered a seventh petition does not matter. But I do feel nonetheless these words deserve special attention: "But deliver us from the evil one." For some reason, the traditional ending—"For yours is the kingdom and the power and the glory forever. Amen"— does not seem to be in the older manuscripts. I do, however, intend to treat that phrase in this book. Furthermore, there is certainly nothing wrong with saying it!

Keep in mind that this final petition, "But deliver us from the evil one," is a part of the plea to be spared an unnecessary pitfall. Although temptation is inevitable, we must not go out looking for it. Although trials are beneficial, it is still wise to avoid them if we can. Persecution is a blessing, yes; and yet Jesus instructed the disciples, "When you are persecuted in one place, flee to another" (Matt. 10:23). If, however, prayer to avoid falling into temptation is not answered, it means we are up to facing it. "Your strength will equal your days" (Deut. 33:25). This explains James 1:2: "Consider it pure joy, my brothers and sisters, whenever you face trials of many kinds." You will treasure what you went through eventually; start considering it pure joy right now. God knows you are equal to the testing. It shows you are strong.

And yet in this extended phrase, "But deliver us from the evil one," we see another reason why Jesus puts this after, "Lead us not into temptation." Why? It is because the devil is obviously behind the pitfall of testing, trial, and temptation. Anything the devil is *in* we should want to avoid. It is the devil who tempts people to sin. It is the devil who brings trouble. When you know that his evil hand is behind what is going on, you want to avoid it with all your might. Do not give him any room—not an inch.

It might be argued that this second clause, "But deliver us from the evil one," is redundant, unnecessary. After all, if we are not led into temptation, we are therefore spared of the evil one. Why did Jesus add this?

The Existence of Evil

By telling us to pray, "Deliver us from the evil one," Jesus has acknowledged that evil is already here. God never explains the origin of evil. We may well wish He had. But had He done so, there would be no need for faith. Nearly every non-Christian I have ever witnessed to for any length of time, especially if he or she is a bit cerebral, asks, "If God exists, why doesn't He stop all the suffering and evil and injustice that is in the world?" It is as if they are saying, "I would believe in God if there were no evil."

I reply: if you knew the answer to that question, there would be no need for faith by any of us. What makes faith

faith is that we do not know why God allows suffering. Why did God create man and woman knowing they would suffer? I don't know. Thank God I don't know, for not knowing is what makes room for faith. It is only by faith that I can be justified (Rom. 4:5), and it is only by faith that I can please God (Heb. 11:6). If the privilege of faith were taken away from me, I would not have any opportunity to be made righteous before God, nor would I have the incalculable joy of pleasing Him.

God sent His Son into the world because evil exists. "The reason the Son of God appeared was to destroy the devil's work" (1 John 3:8). God in His infinite wisdom has chosen to deal with evil in two stages: (1) by sending His one and only Son, Jesus Christ, to die on the cross for our sins; and (2) by the second coming of Jesus, when He appears "from heaven in blazing fire with his powerful angels. He will punish those who do not know God and do not obey the gospel of our Lord Jesus. They will be punished with everlasting destruction and shut out from the presence of the Lord and from the glory of his might on the day he comes to be glorified in his holy people and to be marveled at among all those who have believed" (2 Thess. 1:7–10). This will also result in the ultimate defeat of Satan, who will be thrown into the lake of fire to be tormented day and night forever and ever (Rev. 20:10).

The petition, "But deliver us from the evil one," acknowledges that evil is present; we face it every day. As we pray for daily bread, forgiveness, and not to be led into temptation— essential praying for our spiritual lives—so too must we pray for *daily deliverance*, until the day comes when we are finally delivered by witnessing Satan's total and absolute defeat.

This petition shows that the Christian is in a war. It is

called spiritual warfare. "Be strong in the Lord and in his mighty power. Put on the full armor of God, so that you can take your stand against the devil's schemes. For our struggle is not against flesh and blood, but against the rulers, against the authorities, against the powers of this dark world and against the spiritual forces of evil in the heavenly realms. Therefore put on the full armor of God, so that when the day of evil comes, you may be able to stand your ground, and after you have done everything, to stand" (Eph. 6:10–13).

But do note carefully: these lines show that spiritual warfare is almost entirely *defensive*. You take your "stand." This means you don't go on the attack; you don't go out looking for a chance to pick a fight with Satan. Beware of this. You will get in over your head. Never—ever—initiate a quarrel with the devil. You will fall. But if he attacks you, you will win when you remember Paul's words.

When you were converted, an enemy you did not know you had was awakened. Prior to your conversion you were spiritually blind, for "the god of this age has blinded the minds of unbelievers, so that they cannot see the light of the gospel that displays the glory of Christ, who is the image of God" (2 Cor. 4:4). Every Christian should be reminded: you now have a new enemy—the devil. We must not have a naïve view of life but be wise as serpents, harmless as doves (Matt. 10:16). A solid, sound doctrine of evil is essential both to a good theological foundation and also to practical Christian living.

The Evil One Is the Explanation for All Troubles

Jesus simply stated, "In this world you will have trouble" (John 16:33). We might wish He had not said that. I myself wish He had not said that. I wish He had said, "Because I have appeared on the scene, you will have no more trouble in this world." I wish He had said, "All who follow Me and receive My word will be rewarded by having no problems in this life." I wish Paul had said, "All Christians are exempt from suffering, ill-health, and financial adversity." Mind you, there are preachers abroad who imply this! They mislead people right, left, and center; it is an outrage. Some teach that all people can prosper, all people can be healthy. One popular television preacher even said that if the apostle Paul had had his faith, Paul would not even have had a thorn in the flesh!

Wrong. All of us have thorns in the flesh to some degree. Why? Because in this world there is evil. The devil has not been totally defeated yet. Like it or not, this is the way it is. Why is there trouble in this world? Because of the devil's existence. Why is there temptation? Because there is an evil enemy out there, walking about, seeking whom he may devour (1 Pet. 5:8).

This is why in the Lord's Prayer Jesus did not end with, "Lead us not into temptation," but added, "But deliver us from the evil one." This implicitly shows that Satan is the reason for temptation and trouble in this world. God did not put evil on this earth. God did not put tears in babies' eyes. God did not bring death to His creation. God did not bring suffering and pain.

This is why we want to avoid temptation; we don't want to get near anything Satan is behind. Satan—not God—is the reason for suffering. Satan—not God—is the reason for evil. Satan—not God—is the reason for injustices. Satan—not God—is the explanation for earthquakes, famine, poverty, hatred, racial prejudice, war, corruption in politics, injustice in the banking system, immoral teaching in our schools.

There is therefore a connection between temptation and the devil. The devil is called "the tempter" (1 Thess. 3:5). We saw in the previous chapter that the devil tempted Jesus (Matt. 4:1). He hoped to defeat Jesus before Jesus barely got started in His ministry. He knew who Jesus was: his true enemy. Never forget this: the devil is your enemy and Jesus' enemy. Do not dignify anything the devil puts before you. Stay utterly on the side of Jesus; never—ever—give in to anything that gives pleasure to Satan. Only when God allows you to fall into trials can such trouble be welcomed (Jas. 1:2).

The Essence of Evil

Many of us are used to praying the Lord's Prayer, "Lead us not into temptation, but deliver us from evil"—not "the evil one." But the probable translation is "evil one." The Greek word is *ponerou*—"evil."[1] This word by itself could be masculine or neuter gender. The neuter gender would appear in these verses (all emphases mine): "An evil man brings *evil things* out of the *evil* stored up in his heart" (Luke 6:45). "Hate what is *evil*; cling to what is good" (Rom. 12:9). "Reject every kind of *evil*" (1 Thess. 5:22). These are examples of a neuter gender. The masculine gender, however, appears in the following verses: "When anyone hears the message about the kingdom and does not understand it, *the evil one* comes and snatches away what was sown in their heart" (Matt. 13:19). "The weeds are the people of *the evil one*, and the enemy who sows them is the devil" (Matt. 13:38–39).

Continuing with the aforementioned passage on spiritual

warfare, "In addition to all this, take up the shield of faith, with which you can extinguish all the flaming arrows of *the evil one*" (Eph. 6:16). "Do not be like Cain, who belonged to *the evil one* and murdered his brother" (1 John 3:12). "We know that we are children of God, and that the whole world is under the control of *the evil one*" (1 John 5:19). Also, in this petition in Matthew 6:13 the Greek *tou poverou* shows the definite article—"*the* evil one." Not only that, but the word *apo*—"from"—in "Deliver us *from* evil" almost always refers to a person, not things. I am satisfied that the correct translation is "the evil one," not merely evil.

And yet this phrase in the Lord's Prayer certainly refers to evil generally as well. Evil is in society, the media, government, business, science, medicine, law, the educational systems. Evil refers to how wickedness is compounded when people who hate God and people who hate righteousness unite. King Herod and Pontius Pilate compounded the evil of their day when they approved of the crucifixion of Jesus without a just trial.

There is also a wickedness that would get utterly out of control were it not for common grace. Common grace is God's *special grace in nature* and is the reason the world is not topsy-turvy. When you consider how wicked and unjust the world is, have you ever wondered why it isn't worse than it is? Answer: God's common grace, His goodness to all men. It has nothing to do directly with salvation; it is God's general goodness to everybody. The reason we have hospitals, doctors, nurses, laws, traffic lights, and government is due to common grace. The reason people have talents, intelligence, abilities, and motivation to do good is owing to common grace. You could have a high level of common grace and compose a Grieg's Concerto in A Minor, be an

Albert Einstein with an IQ over 200, or play the piano like Arthur Rubinstein and not be a Christian or even moral. Common grace explains how God rules the world generally: showing His goodness to everybody, whether they are believers or not. All who are converted had common grace before they came to faith; but not all who have common grace—even a high level of ability—come to faith. This common grace maintains a certain control in the world lest things get totally out of hand. Common grace even keeps a lid on wickedness to a high degree, or things would be infinitely worse than they are.

What, then, does Jesus tell us about the devil? Four things: (1) that he is there—he exists, (2) that he is evil—totally wicked, (3) that he is active—alive and well, (4) that he is still under God's control. Satan is not all-powerful; God is. Otherwise, Jesus would not have given this petition. The reason we can pray for daily deliverance from the evil one is because God is greater than the devil. God even allows the devil to promote His purposes in the world.

Examples of Evil

Let's examine ways we face the evil one every day. I said he is active. What does he do?

First, the devil loves to terrorize. That is his specialty. It is what he does. All of us at times fear. He is the author of fear. He implants fear. He wants to make you fear and live in utter anxiety. Are you afraid? Do you live in fear? Are you motivated all the time by a spirit of fear? If so, the devil has succeeded with you to some extent. Being afraid is exactly what the devil wants of you. Satan works through fear. One of his nicknames is "accuser of our brothers and sisters" (Rev.

12:10). He works by fear and through fear, so Paul assured us that God has not given us a spirit of fear (2 Tim. 1:7). The more you are set free from fear, the greater your strength when Satan attempts to terrorize you.

Know this about the devil: he is a liar. "When he lies, he speaks his native language, for he is a liar and the father of lies," said Jesus (John 8:44). When he accuses you, it is often to make you think you are evil, unworthy, and not justified in calling yourself a Christian. He will also point out things about you that are true—to bring you down, reminding you of your faults and failures. This is why the great theologian William Perkins said not to believe the devil, "even when he tells the truth"!

Second, the devil's job is to tempt. As we saw already in this chapter, he is called the tempter; he tempted Jesus in the desert. But his style is to work through our weaknesses. The devil knows us better than we know ourselves. He is shrewd, clever, canny, crafty. He has a computer printout on your nature, habits, past, and lifestyle and knows exactly how to bring you down by exploiting your weakness. He works through our natural weakness to achieve his end: our downfall.

There are basically three ways he seeks to defeat us:

(1) *Through pride.* Pride is at the bottom of all hate and unforgiveness. Do not forget 2 Corinthians 2:11: a good reason to forgive is to keep from being outsmarted by the devil. While it may be anger that makes us lose our temper; our pride *keeps* us angry. We hate to admit we are wrong. It is what makes us jealous; we cannot bear another's success. He appeals to your ambition and self-esteem to make you stumble. "Pride goes before destruction, a haughty spirit

141

before a fall" (Prov. 16:18). Our fall through pride is the devil's work.

(2) *Through sexual temptation.* We dealt with this in the previous chapter. But let me add that Satan loves to achieve success by getting a Christian, especially a leader, to fall; it brings disgrace upon the name of Christ and gives the world a chance to mock the church. Pride is also at the bottom of sexual temptation; we are flattered by compliments, we need our esteem to be empowered. Satan knows this. My loving and earnest counsel to you, dear reader: have such an esteem for God's glory and a care for another's life that you would not want to bring shame upon God's name or pain to another person.

Sexual sin will lead to the greatest possible regret. Don't let it happen to you. And if as you read these lines you are in an affair, stop it! Or are considering an affair, stop it! *And stop it now.* Don't give the devil an opportunity; make no provision that he can work through your sexual desires (Rom. 13:14).

(3) *Through unbelief.* Satan began to tempt Jesus by saying, "If you are the Son of God," trying to impart a doubt that maybe He wasn't (Matt. 4:3). He did this with Eve in the Garden of Eden: "Did God really say, 'You must not eat from any tree in the garden'?" (Gen. 3:1). The first thing the devil did was to implant doubt in Eve's mind that God did not say what He said—and also to twist God's word. For God never said for her not to eat of "any" tree but only the tree of the knowledge of good and evil (Gen. 2:17). The devil wants to make you doubt—your salvation, the Bible, God's love for you, His plans for you. Resist the devil, and he will flee from you (Jas. 4:7).

Third, the devil wants to test us. He is the great counterfeiter.

"Satan himself masquerades as an angel of light" (2 Cor. 11:14). The devil plays into our lack of discernment, even into our desire to be godly. He will set up false prophets and unscrupulous ministers to divert us from the truth. He hates truth. He hates good teaching. He hates the gospel of Christ. He hates a true exposition of the Bible. When Christians are not knowledgeable in the Scriptures, they are easy targets for the devil to bring down. "My people are destroyed from lack of knowledge" (Hos. 4:6).

The more we develop a sense of discernment, the more we will be able to recognize the true presence of God, and the more we will be able to recognize the counterfeit. Don't try to be an expert in what is counterfeit. Don't read up on all the cults and false doctrines; get to know the Bible so well and the presence of God so well that you can instantly tell when the false lifts up its ugly head.

These are examples you and I will face to some degree every day. If we can anticipate the devil's setup in these three areas—terrorizing, tempting, and testing—we will not likely be taken by surprise. We therefore pray daily that we will be spared. Remember, the devil never sleeps. He works day and night—in your dreams when you sleep (if he can) and in broad daylight through all I have just said. I also think of something my father used to say to me over and over again: "The devil is very crafty, second only to God in power and wisdom."

Deliverance From Evil

There are degrees of the need for deliverance. The most serious level is to be demonized or even demon-possessed. It is when one comes under the devil's domain and seems helpless. Such a person may desire to be out of their misery but is powerless. How many readers will need to think along this line when praying "Lead us not into temptation, but deliver us from the evil one" I do not know; but I feel I cannot ignore this possibility.

There are two extremes when it comes to the study of the devil. One is to ignore him entirely—to deny that he exists (which he loves). The other is to be preoccupied with him and see a demon on every bush (which he also loves). I worry about those who have a preoccupation with spiritual warfare and seem to want to become "experts" in this area. I sometimes think they have more fear of Satan than they have trust in the power of God. Is it not interesting too that Jesus waited until the end of the Lord's Prayer to mention the devil?

There is, however, a most neglected kind of exorcism— and do you know what it is? It is called total forgiveness. You can look high and low across the continent for the person who is supposedly filled with the most power to cast out devils and be disappointed. But if you forgive—totally— I can promise you that the devil will make his exodus as you bless your enemy and refuse to seek any vengeance. I don't rule out those who have a ministry of deliverance, but if you are filled with bitterness and expect the demon to exit under another's gifting, you are going to be disappointed.

I recommend truly forgiving that person who mistreated you—forgive them where you are right now. You may need a wise person to counsel you as well (this could be very important), but there is a deep well to be explored that is right under your nose. Defeat the devil by total forgiveness. I will have more to say about this a bit later.

The Three Rs of Spiritual Warfare

Remember the "three Rs" of spiritual warfare: recognize, refuse, resist. First, *recognize* that it is the evil one at work. This is not always easy to do. Spiritual discernment is a gift of the Holy Spirit (1 Cor. 12:10). But it does not follow that you need this particular gift to recognize the devil. When you are terrorized by fear, when the temptation is vehement, when the testing is overpowering—count on it: this is the devil. That is the first step in spiritual warfare: recognize the devil when he molests you, diverts you from godly thoughts, makes you lose concentration when you pray or read the Bible.

Second, *refuse*. This may not be easy. But do your best to *refuse to think* about the thoughts he puts in your mind. For example, when you get a strong urge to doubt God's love, it is the devil; refuse to dignify these thoughts. In a word, refuse to think about anything that is not wholesome. "Whatever is true, whatever is noble, whatever is right, whatever is pure, whatever is lovely, whatever is admirable—if anything is excellent or praiseworthy—think about such things" (Phil. 4:8). When the devil puts a negative thought in your head, refuse to think about it.

Third, *resist*. This means to persevere in refusing to listen to him. Resist. Resist. Resist. When the devil sees you are not going to give in to his cunning ways, he will leave you. That is the teaching of the New Testament. "Submit yourselves, then, to God. Resist the devil, and he will flee from you" (Jas. 4:7). "Be alert and of sober mind. Your enemy the devil prowls around like a roaring lion looking for someone to devour. Resist him, standing firm in the faith, because you know that the family of believers throughout the world is undergoing the same kind of sufferings" (1 Pet. 5:8–9).

Remember too that a characteristic of a lion is to *roar*. This is so his prey will suppose they are defeated before the lion even starts! The devil is like this. He roars to make you think you don't have a chance, that you may as well give in. Wrong. Resist him. He will flee. As Martin Luther put it, "One little word shall fell him."[2] The lion's roar is meant to scare you, to make you dread today, tomorrow, your future. He is a liar; recognize, refuse, resist.

What I have said in this chapter should hopefully bring some coherence to this petition, "Lead us not into temptation, but deliver us from the evil one." It means a daily deliverance. You need it today. You will need it again tomorrow. This is not the same thing as demon possession; deliverance regarding being demonized may be a one-off matter. But apart from that, you will need a victory over the devil every day—over fear, over sexual temptation, and over testing of your faith. It is a daily matter. Expect it. Don't be surprised that you need to pray this petition often—and do all you can to act upon it, as we saw in the previous chapter. "Watch and pray" (Matt. 26:41).

The End of Evil

The Lord's Prayer will eventually be answered in full. You will ultimately be totally delivered from the devil. When Jesus comes the second time, it will spell Satan's final end. Until then, we will need a daily deliverance.

The devil knows his end. The demons shouted at Jesus, "What do You want of us, You Son of God? Have You come here to make us suffer before it is our time to suffer?"

(Matt. 8:29). Many translations call this the "appointed time." The appointed time signals an eschatological event—in the future—when Satan and all his fallen angels will be punished. They know this is coming. The Lord Jesus will destroy the devil "with the breath of his mouth and destroy [the devil] by the splendor of his coming" (2 Thess. 2:8). When Satan was overcome by the blood of the Lamb, the admonition came: "Therefore rejoice, you heavens and you who dwell in them! But woe to the earth and the sea, because the devil has gone down to you! He is filled with fury, because he knows that his time is short" (Rev. 12:12). Yes. His time is short. He will not always be around. As someone has said, "The next time the devil reminds you of your past, remind him of his future!"

We never outgrow praying the Lord's Prayer this side of heaven. We don't outgrow one single petition, as if to say, "Well, I won't need to pray that again." Sorry, but you will need to pray this as long as you live. Yet one day God will command His angel to sound the trumpet. "For the Lord himself will come down from heaven, with a loud command, with the voice of the archangel and with the trumpet call of God, and the dead in Christ will rise first" (1 Thess. 4:16). "In a flash, in the twinkling of an eye, at the last trumpet. For the trumpet will sound, the dead will be raised imperishable, and we will be changed" (1 Cor. 15:52). When that day comes, you can count on it: "So we will be with the Lord forever" (1 Thess. 4:17).

We won't be praying the Lord's Prayer in heaven! This prayer will have been completely answered by then. So pray it now!

PART 4

A CHOSEN BENEDICTION

CHAPTER 11

THE KINGDOM, THE POWER, AND THE GLORY

For Yours is the kingdom and the power
and the glory forever. Amen.
—MATTHEW 6:13, NKJV

THERE IS SOME doubt whether this final phrase of the Lord's Prayer was in the original Greek New Testament—and for that matter in Jesus' teaching (He spoke in Aramaic). It is thought that some people in the church added this benediction, or blessing, to close the prayer and that the words were incorporated in later manuscripts. But also keep in mind that it is very possible indeed that these were the actual words of Jesus. One thing is quite certain: many of us have prayed these beautiful words—and I myself shall continue to do so. After all, the words are *absolutely true*, even if Jesus did not say them. And if we repeat these words when we pray the Lord's Prayer, it certainly would be good to know what we are saying!

The origin of this phrase goes back to King David. When David praised the Lord in the presence of the whole assembly, he said:

> Praise be to you, LORD, the God of our father Israel, from everlasting to everlasting. Yours, LORD, is the greatness and the power and the glory and the majesty and the splendor, for everything in heaven and earth is yours. Yours, LORD, is the kingdom; you are exalted as head over all. Wealth and honor come from you; you are the ruler of all things. In your hands are strength and power to exalt and give strength to all. Now, our God, we give you thanks, and praise your glorious name.
>
> —1 CHRONICLES 29:10–13

This is a wonderful statement of praise. A summary of King David's words of adoration bring the Lord's Prayer to a magnificent benediction: "Yours is the kingdom and the power and the glory forever. Amen." Many people say, "Forever *and ever*. Amen."

The Kingdom

When David said, *"Yours, Lord, is the kingdom*; you are exalted as head over all"* (1 Chron. 29:11, emphasis mine), this was Israel's king acknowledging the kingship of God. King David humbly and rightly acknowledged that he himself was under God, Israel's true King. Every existing monarch in the world should do this. "I am your King," God wanted Israel to know and never forget (Isa. 43:15). Therefore, King David makes up for Israel's failure. They demanded their own king, to be like other nations (1 Sam. 8:19–20). God acquiesced and told Samuel to let them have their way (1 Sam. 8:7, 9, 22). God granted their request but sent leanness into their souls (Ps. 106:15, KJV).

What Israel failed to affirm, then—that God was their

true King—King David made up for. He was careful never to forget that God was his and Israel's King. He refused to take himself seriously, as King Saul did. Saul became "yesterday's man," as I describe in my book *The Anointing*. We too will become yesterday's men or women if we take ourselves too seriously, promoting ourselves to the level of a calling that did not come from God. We can know we are today's men and women to the degree the Holy Spirit rules in us ungrieved. Therefore before all Israel David proclaimed, "Yours, LORD, is the kingdom; you are exalted as head over all" (1 Chron. 29:11).

When we repeat the words "Yours is the kingdom," we affirm not only that God our heavenly Father is our King but also that the kingdom *belongs to Him*. It is His, not ours; He shares it with us as He is pleased to do. Jesus said of those who are poor in spirit, "Theirs is the kingdom of heaven" (Matt. 5:3). He also said it of those who are persecuted for the cause of Jesus Christ: "Theirs is the kingdom of heaven" (Matt. 5:10). This does not mean that they own it, or that they are in charge, as if they were the head. No. But it does mean that they *inherit* the kingdom by God's sovereign pleasure and are given a special consciousness of the very real presence of God. Jesus said, "Do not be afraid, little flock, for your Father has been pleased to give you the kingdom" (Luke 12:32).

When Jesus said, "Ask and it will be given to you; seek and you will find; knock and the door will be opened to you" (Matt. 7:7), He primarily was referring to our receiving the kingdom. To inherit and enjoy the kingdom is what Jesus is emphasizing in the Sermon on the Mount. Many people take Matthew 7:7 out of context and apply it to almost everything they have a wish for, and God may even accommodate them. But the context of Matthew 7:7 is that we will be hungry for God and thirsting after the righteousness Jesus described. To those who want this, Jesus simply says, "Ask for it, and you will receive it." Yes, it is the Father's good pleasure to give us the kingdom.

However, we must also remember that the kingdom of God is to be understood in more than one way. When you and I pray, "Yours is the kingdom," we too need to incorporate more than one meaning simultaneously.

The saintly Scottish preacher Robert Murray M'Cheyne (1813–1843) reckoned that our Lord Jesus Christ wears two crowns: one pertaining to the state, one pertaining to the church. This was M'Cheyne's way of saying that God is both ruler over the nations and head of the church. He is Lord over the political realm, of government and all those issues we saw earlier regarding "common grace." God is sovereign over all—everybody and everything. This means He is in charge of all elections; He puts people in office. "The authorities that exist have been established by God" (Rom. 13:1). We can pray for our personal choices and vote according to our consciences, but at the end of the day *God decides*.

However, a nation that does not acknowledge that God is supreme over it, and does not believe that the nation is blessed whose God is the Lord (Ps. 33:12), may inherit evil rulers who will bring calamity and misery to a country. This is why the church should pray that God will overrule and give us not what we deserve but what is best for us.

So too is our Lord Jesus the head of the church. "He is the head of the body, the church" (Col. 1:18). The buck stops with Him. All church hierarchy, church politics, church officers, pastoral leadership, and members are under the headship of Jesus Christ. But if a church strays from the gospel and the revealed will of God—the Bible—that church will lose its right to exist. It will be as Paul foretold long ago: "having a form of godliness but denying its power" (2 Tim. 3:5). That is when the church becomes an empty shell. King Jesus has the right to remove a church's lampstand from its place, as He warned (Rev. 2:5). This means that a church will lose its anointing or, the worst possible scenario, become apostate (fallen, in utter powerlessness and disgrace).

At the same time, it does not necessarily mean that a church is wiped off the map, although this can happen too; it mainly means that a church can have a name that it lives but is in fact "dead" (Rev. 3:1). Someone has said that if the Holy Spirit were taken completely from the church today, 90 percent of its work would carry on as if nothing had happened.

The church is God's visible vehicle for expressing kingdom power. "His intent was that now, through the church, the manifold wisdom of God should be made known…according to his eternal purpose that he accomplished in Christ Jesus our Lord" (Eph. 3:10–11). You and I are a part of this visible instrument. Therefore, when you and I utter the words "Yours is the kingdom," we represent the church. But in these words we also affirm God's jurisdiction over the whole world. We acknowledge that Jesus Christ is our Supreme Head but are at the same time following David in acknowledging the sovereign rule of God over all the earth. And as the Lord's Prayer is addressed to the Father, we are therefore honoring Him as being the absolute Lord of heaven and earth—and over our own lives. We bow to Him. He is our sovereign, our monarch. He is the great King "than which nothing greater can be conceived."[1]

This benediction therefore acknowledges that God is the

One who rules the world, the nations, and the church—and can replace rulers, heads of state, and ecclesiastical leaders. "No one from the east or the west or from the desert can exalt themselves. It is God who judges: He brings one down, he exalts another" (Ps. 75:6–7). As Hosea said later, referring to the generation that demanded a king, "So in my anger I gave you a king, and in my wrath I took him away" (Hos. 13:11).

Finally, to utter the words "Yours is the kingdom" is to honor and accept His verdict regarding our own inheritance in the kingdom. God said to Moses, "I will have mercy on whom I will have mercy, and I will have compassion on whom I will have compassion" (Exod. 33:19). We cannot twist God's arm and make Him immediately give us this great sense of His presence. It is His good pleasure to give it to us—but in His timing and on His terms. To say "Yours is the kingdom" is to stop snapping our fingers at God and expecting Him to act at our command.

When Jesus told Peter how the apostle would die, Peter wanted to know God's will for John as well. But in so many words Jesus said, "That's none of your business—you just follow Me and don't worry about John." (See John 21:18–22.) God has a particular, special, and individual will for each of us. "He chose our inheritance for us" (Ps. 47:4). We may wish to look over our shoulders curiously to see what God has decided for others around us. But He says, "Stop looking at others and follow Me." We have enough to do merely to walk in the light God has given to *us*, not others. When we say, "Yours is the kingdom," we are agreeing to do just that!

The Power

"Yours is the kingdom and the power." The power in these words refers to the Holy Spirit. There are at least two Greek words that can be translated "power": *dunamis*[2] (enabling) and *exousia*[3] (authority). The word here is *dunamis*—the enabling energy or power that makes things happen. Jesus might have used either or both words, but He used *dunamis*, from which we get the word *dynamite*. Therefore, when we say, "Yours is the power," we refer to the Holy Spirit's power. It is the word Jesus used when He said to the disciples before His ascension, "Stay in the city until you have been clothed with power from on high" (Luke 24:49). "You will receive power when the Holy Spirit comes on you; and you will be my witnesses in Jerusalem, and in all Judea and Samaria, and to the ends of the earth" (Acts 1:8).

The point here is that only the enabling power of the Spirit can make the kingdom real to us. To say "Yours is the power" is to confess our helplessness without that power. This power can sometimes be used interchangeably with anointing. It is what opens our eyes, dispels the blindness, and enables us to understand truth. It is what gives us insight into Holy Scripture. It is what helps us overcome fear. It is what gives us confidence when we talk to others about Jesus Christ. It was the power of the Holy Spirit that enabled the disciples to witness in Jerusalem, Judea, et al. Peter did not believe Jesus when he was told he would deny Christ (Mark 14:29–31). But he was an utter coward hours later before a servant girl and indeed denied even knowing Jesus (Mark 14:66–72).

How could Peter do this and be so weak? It was because he was left to himself and filled with fear; he was empty of strength and confidence within himself. In a word: he was devoid of the Spirit's power. He was so sure he would be strong within himself and sincerely thought he would never deny Jesus. But he did.

However, on the day of Pentecost, Peter was as bold as a lion, preaching with power, liberty, confidence, and authority before thousands of fellow Jews—and he startled them all. Instead of mocking and laughing at Peter, his hearers were "cut to the heart" and pleaded, "What shall we do?" (Acts 2:37).

It was power that the person had in mind when he said that if the Holy Spirit were completely taken from the church today, 90 percent of the church's work would continue as if nothing had happened. This is the meaning of those words "having a form of godliness but denying its power" (2 Tim. 3:5). Paul also said to Timothy that God has not given us a spirit of fear but "of power, love and self-discipline" (2 Tim. 1:7).

Many Christians today seem to be afraid of the Holy Spirit. There are denominations whose doctrine of the Trinity could be summed up, "God the Father, God the Son, and God the Holy Bible." They have the Bible but not the Spirit's power. They are sound in many ways but are so cold, formal, and seemingly lifeless, demonstrating a 10 percent reliance on the Holy Spirit.

I was born and raised in Kentucky. A century before I was born, a phenomenon known as "camp meetings" emerged in Bourbon County, Kentucky, just over a hundred miles from the Nazarene church in my hometown of Ashland. Thousands came to a place called Cane Ridge in Bourbon County in their covered wagons from several states, representing various denominations. On a Sunday morning at

Cane Ridge in July 1801, a Methodist lay preacher stood on a fallen tree, taking his text from 2 Corinthians 5:10: "For we must all appear before the judgment seat of Christ; that every one may receive the things done in his body, according to that he hath done, whether it be good or bad" (kjv).

An estimated fifteen thousand people had gathered to hear him preach. When he finished, hundreds of people lay prostrate on the ground, seemingly unconscious. For the next several days there was never a time but that at least five hundred people were flat out on the ground. A bit of panic set in, and some thought they were dead. But after a few hours these same people would revive with loud shouts of assurance of salvation. It was like "the sound of Niagara," someone said, referring to the noise of the people, which could be heard a mile away. Some cynical, mocking people would make their way to scoff at the happenings, only to be smote and converted when they reached Cane Ridge. Now known as the Cane Ridge Revival, it is regarded as America's Second Great Awakening.

There is no valid natural explanation for this—only the power of the Spirit. This is what it must have been like immediately after Peter preached. Only the power of the Spirit can cause thousands to be converted in hours. Only the power of the Spirit can cause people who are opinionated, blind, cold, and hard—and apparently unreachable—to become soft, tender, open, and eager to do whatever God prompts them to do.

Dr. and Mrs. Martyn Lloyd-Jones used to talk to me about the Welsh Revival and stories that came from it. Mrs. Lloyd-Jones was actually present in Wales for a while to see it. Her father took her out of school in London and put her on a train at Paddington Station for her to go to Wales in 1904. He was criticized for taking her out of school. He replied, "She can always go to school, but she may never see revival again."

Dr. Lloyd-Jones told me of a coal miner who was thoroughly annoyed with his wife for not cooking his meal when he got home from work. She was at the local church instead, enthralled with the Welsh Revival. He could take it no more. Determined to make a scene and end the revival meetings, he went straight to the church. But he could not get in because of the crowds of people around the door. So he pushed his way through those at the door and made his way to the back pew of the church. The next thing he remembered was finding himself on his knees in front of the pulpit crying out to God to save him. Those present said he stood on the back pew, then stepped on the back of each pew, one at a time, toward the pulpit until he fell at the front of the church—in submission to God. That is the kind of power that was present in Wales during that time.

You cannot manufacture this kind of power. You cannot work it up. You cannot legislate it. You cannot make it happen. It belongs to God. "Yours is the power." And yet I fear this is what is missing in the church at the present time. The absence of this power is the explanation for long altar calls, trying to plead people into moving. It is the explanation for the absence of gospel preaching, appealing to people's self-interest instead. It is the reason the church's influence is minimal in so many countries at the present time and why people don't take the church seriously. It is why there is little fear of God in the world today. It is why people blaspheme God and godliness right, left, and center, with no worry that there is a God in heaven who sees and hears.

You cannot force God to open your own eyes or anyone

else's. You may open your Bible to read it and pray for guidance and insight. But unless the Spirit comes on you, you will read and read with no spiritual understanding. The Bible is a spiritual book. It is not like reading a book on architecture, psychology, philosophy, history, literature, or even theology. You can read these disciplines and understand what you read. But not the Bible. The greatest intellect cannot grasp the true meaning of Scripture at the natural level. He or she may say, "It makes no sense to me," thinking it is their great brain that dismisses the truth of God's Word. But should the Spirit come upon a person, whether that man or woman is educated or simple, God's Word will be clear, brilliant, and full of insight.

Jesus told the disciples to tarry—to wait for this power to come. We need to do this today. We must not settle for anything less. God is sovereign and has a will of His own. But He has also encouraged us to pray for this power. We should go to Him on bended knee. Yes, pray the Lord's Prayer on bended knee. And remember that it is the Holy Spirit who is meant when we say, "Yours is the power."

The Glory

"Yours is the kingdom and the power and the glory." This mainly means that we must not forget to give God the credit for what He does should He answer any of the petitions in the Lord's Prayer. We must always give Him the credit if He answers any of our prayers. We never have a right to pat ourselves on the back and think that any success or answer to our prayers is due to our perseverance or faithfulness, although God wants us never to give up. God gets all the glory—the credit—for what is done.

As the phrase *kingdom of God* can be explained accurately in several ways, so too this word *glory*. This to me is an exciting study. I have been enthralled with this word for over fifty years and am still trying to understand it.

In the Old Testament, the Hebrew word is *kabodh*[4] (also spelled *kabod*). One of its meanings is "heaviness." We may say of someone today, "He or she is a heavyweight," meaning they are not common or ordinary but have a lot of importance— like a senator, member of parliament, or bishop. We use the expression that someone "throws their weight around"—like an officer in the military or a political or even ecclesiastical figure. That is the idea of the *kabodh*.

The God of the Bible is a God of glory. But this heaviness can also be almost physical, even visible. When the ark of the covenant was brought into the temple for the first time, the temple was "filled with the cloud, and the priests could not perform their service because of the cloud, for the *glory of the Lord* filled the temple of God" (2 Chron. 5:13–14, emphasis mine).

One should wish that the glory of God would come into a church so that the entire proceedings were disrupted and all plans had to be suspended. I used to see this at times when I was a boy growing up in my old church in Ashland. I have seen the presence and power of God build up over a time so powerfully that people stood up and ran to the front to pray before the preacher could finish his sermon—and he would stop preaching. I have sometimes thought that perhaps a touch of the Cane Ridge Revival was still around in Ashland in my earliest days. I do know that they called us Nazarenes "Noisy-renes"!

The New Testament word for glory is *doxa*,[5] from which we get *doxology*. It means "praise." But it comes from a root

word that actually means "opinion." This is very important. God has an opinion. As a matter of fact, He has an
opinion on everything! Furthermore, He wants to share His
opinion—and for us to take it seriously. This is because He
wants praise and glory for every idea He has, every opinion
He shares.

The verse I have sought to be governed by is John 5:44,
for me the most important verse in the Bible, which I read
every day to myself: "How can you believe, if you accept
praise from one another and don't seek the praise that comes
from the only God?" (NET). I was introduced to this verse in
the King James Version: "How can ye believe, which receive
honour one of another, and seek not the honour that cometh
from God only?" This is the way I learned the verse. I am
glad it reads as it does, hinting that it is God's praise *alone*—
"God only"—that matters. That is the way I understood the
verse from the beginning. I grew to want only His honor,
not that which comes from people—and to be motivated by
this alone.

This verse uncovers the reason the Jews missed their
Messiah. They were locked into wanting one another's praise
so much that when their own promised Messiah showed up
under their noses, they missed Him entirely. Surprise, surprise, said Jesus: "How *can* you believe?" Jesus was implying,
"You can't." It would be impossible to believe when they were
preoccupied with praise for one another without making any
effort to seek the praise that comes from the true and only
God. That is how they missed what God was doing in their
day; it is why we can miss what God is doing in our day too.

Jonathan Edwards taught us that the task of every generation is to discover in which direction the sovereign
Redeemer is moving, then move in that direction. But if

we are consumed with the wish to have praise from one another—making no effort to seek God's praise—we too will miss what God is up to in our day, as the Jews missed it two thousand years ago.

God is a jealous God. His name is Jealous (Exod. 34:14). As a consequence of this, He resents it when He does not get all the glory for what He does. Like it or not, that is the way He is. And when we pray the Lord's Prayer, concluding with "Yours is the kingdom and the power and the glory," we are promising *not to forget* to give Him all the glory!

Do you? Do you give Him all the glory for what He does? The worst mistake you and I could make is to underestimate how much God wants all the credit for what He does. Don't even come close—not even an inch—to elbowing in on His glory. It is a scary thing to do. And yet we must all be taught this. That is precisely what Jesus was doing when He gave us the Lord's Prayer. And whether it was Jesus or the church that gave us these words, "Yours is the kingdom and the power and the glory," they are absolutely true. We are impoverished if we neglect them—and wonderfully blessed if we take them very seriously indeed.

"Forever. Amen."

The intent here is that God wants us to remember that the kingdom is eternally and irrevocably His, that the power always comes from Him (and not from within us), and that the glory must always go to Him. This is an unchangeable, eternal truth and principle. "I the LORD do not change" (Mal. 3:6). "Jesus Christ is the same yesterday and today and forever" (Heb. 13:8).

Amen[6] is an Aramaic word that means "so be it." We use

amen to endorse another's prayer; we say it at the end of our own prayers, as if to confirm we mean what we just said.

With these brief closing comments, my exposition on the Lord's Prayer is finished. Moreover, this might have ended the book. But our Lord isn't quite finished yet, so neither am I. We turn now to His final observation regarding this prayer.

PART 5

A FURTHER
REASON FOR THE
LORD'S PRAYER

CHAPTER 12

JESUS' P.S. TO THE LORD'S PRAYER

For if you forgive other people when they sin
against you, your heavenly Father will also
forgive you. But if you do not forgive others their
sins, your Father will not forgive your sins.

—MATTHEW 6:14–15

BECAUSE OF THESE glaring two words, "for if" (*ean gar*[1] in Greek), immediately following the prayer Jesus gave to us, we instantly see that He has purposefully not changed the subject yet. Although He did not apparently add this P.S. when He gave the prayer to the disciples in Luke 11:2–4, He certainly reveals He is not finished with this prayer in the Sermon on the Mount. He clearly has more to say about the Lord's Prayer before He moves on in the Sermon on the Mount.

When Jesus included the petition "Forgive us our debts [sins], as we also have forgiven our debtors [those who have sinned against us]" (Matt. 6:12) in the Lord's Prayer, it was not the first time He taught this in the Sermon on the Mount. The first indication was in Matthew 5:7: "Blessed are the merciful, for they will be shown mercy." It was further implied in His stunning teaching that hate was the same as murder in Matthew 5:21–22, but in Matthew 5:44 He clearly said: "Love your enemies and pray for those who persecute you." He added, "Be perfect, therefore, as your heavenly Father is perfect" (Matt. 5:48). He wants us to forgive as the Father forgives.

From this general context it might be argued that Jesus' chief reason for giving the Lord's Prayer in the first place was to teach love and forgiveness again. If so, this is why He stated at the end of the prayer, "For if you forgive other people when they sin against you, your heavenly Father will also forgive you" (Matt. 6:14). However, I am sure there were many reasons—not merely forgiveness—He gave us the Lord's Prayer. The immediate context is about prayer—showing what prayer ought not to be and what it should be (Matt. 6:5–8), whereupon He gave us the Lord's Prayer. You may recall that the context in Luke 11 was in response to the disciples' request, "Lord, teach us to pray" (v. 1).

In any case, Jesus could have moved on to another subject in the Sermon on the Mount as soon as He finished giving the prayer itself. But He didn't. He had more to say on the matter and referred to only one of the petitions, namely, the petition that said, "Forgive us our debts, as we also have forgiven our debtors" (Matt. 6:12).

He apparently considered this the most important of the petitions, and the one that needed the most attention.

Does this surprise you? The truth is, the teaching of forgiveness is the greatest need of the church today. Until fairly recently, nearly all books on forgiveness related to God forgiving us, and almost none focused on the subject of our forgiving others. Jesus' teaching on this is plain as day, but we all have a way of sweeping it under the carpet. I myself did—for years and years. Until one day, in my darkest hour, Josef Tson had the courage to say to me, "RT, you must totally forgive them; until you totally forgive them, you will be in chains. Release them, and you will be released." Nobody had ever talked to me that way in my life. "Faithful are the wounds of a friend" (Prov. 27:6, KJV). How I thank God for Josef Tson.

All I know is, Jesus returns to the subject. He will not let us off the hook. Someone has said, "The truth which makes us free is for the most part the truth which we prefer not to hear." How true. Is there anything more painful than being told we must let those who have hurt us totally off the hook and even pray God's blessing upon them? Can *anything* be harder than that? Probably not. But it is certainly the most emancipating teaching there is.

If Jesus did not change the subject, I felt I too must not close my book on the Lord's Prayer just yet either. I therefore feel I have a duty to deal with Matthew 6:13–14, even briefly, before the book is complete.

I will say it again. As for the teaching on total forgiveness, you and I can never get enough of it. I need it as much as ever. As a matter of fact, almost twenty years ago I took upon myself a discipline to read Luke 6:37 every day: "Do not judge, and you will not be judged. Do not condemn, and you will not be condemned. Forgive, and you will be forgiven." Why do I read this regularly? Because I need it so much. My weakness is to judge. I need to be reminded all the time to be gentle and button my lip when the temptation is to criticize or find fault. We point the finger because we do not totally forgive. If we totally forgive, the need to judge evaporates like water in the tropical sun. Reading this verse regularly has been very, very helpful to me personally. The heart is deceitful (Jer. 17:9); we think we have mastered the art of totally forgiving, only to discover we failed yet again.

I am convinced this is why Jesus did not change the subject when He finished the Lord's Prayer. He knew the disciples needed it and that the church would need it. The truth is we all need it.

The Foundation for a Greater Anointing

How many of us have realized that when Jesus said, "Whatever you ask for in prayer, believe that you *have received it*, and it will be yours," He didn't stop there? He added: "And when you stand praying, if you hold anything against anyone, forgive them, so that your Father in heaven may forgive you your sins" (Mark 11:24–25, emphasis mine). Believing that you have received what you pray for is a very high level of faith indeed. As a matter of fact, it is God's faith—the faith of God. Jesus actually introduced this by saying, "Have faith in God," but the Greek reads *ei echete pistin theou*—literally, "If you have faith of God" (Mark 11:22, as in the margin of some editions of the KJV). I will only observe that saying to a mountain, "Go, throw yourself into the sea" (Mark 11:23), and not doubting it will happen is given only to those who have a supernatural level of faith.

Whether the scholars translate *pistin theou* as faith "in" God or faith "of" God is for them to decide. I will only ask: When is the last time you heard of someone speaking to a mountain to have it cast into the sea? Only God can do that. And yet Jesus encouraged us to have this kind of faith.

My point is this section is concluded by Jesus' word about forgiveness: "If you hold anything against anyone [when you stand praying], forgive them, so that your Father in heaven may forgive you your sins" (v. 25). Whether anyone has ever caused a mountain to fall into the sea, one thing is for certain: Jesus is showing we should not even *expect* to have faith like that unless we have totally forgiven all those who have sinned against us.

The prerequisite for having the kind of faith as described in Mark 11:22–25 is total forgiveness. It is the only way forward for a greater anointing. It is probably the most neglected teaching when it comes to the need for power and seeing the miraculous. Giving millions to the church will not do it. Giving to the poor won't do it. Giving your body to be burned won't do it (1 Cor. 13:3, ESV). A forty-day fast will not do it. Total forgiveness is what is required. It is God's faith we should pray for: to forgive "just as in Christ *God forgave you*" (Eph. 4:32, emphasis mine).

I have long admired and wanted to be like Stephen, a truly great hero portrayed in the New Testament. His opponents could not resist the wisdom or the Spirit by whom he spoke. What an anointing he had! His face shone like that of an angel (Acts 6:10, 15). What do you suppose was the key—the explanation for such an anointing? I answer: he was devoid of all bitterness. When he was dying from being stoned by his persecutors, his last words were, "Do not hold this sin against them" (Acts 7:60). What a way to die!

We all have hurts. We all have a story to tell. Jesus knows that. This is why He says "when" in Matthew 6:14. "If you forgive other people *when* [not *if*] they sin against you" (emphasis mine). It is only a matter of time until someone will hurt us, lie about us, falsely accuse us, be jealous of us, neglect us, perhaps physically hurt us, not keep their word to us, possibly be unfaithful to us, embarrass us, take advantage of us, totally let us down and disappoint us, shock us, walk all over us, and if possible, abuse us. Jesus' teaching is so practical—and possible to apply. We may like to think it is not possible, but it is. We simply have to keep doing it when we fail.

Totally forgiving those who have been unjust is to let them completely, utterly, and totally off the hook—and then pray (sincerely) that God will bless them! "That's hard," you say. Yes. It is hard. But it is required of you and me to do. Why should we do it? We do it because we take Jesus' word seriously, because we want to inherit the kingdom, and because we want to be conscious of His manifest presence as much as possible. And also we forgive because we don't want to be outsmarted by Satan (2 Cor. 2:10–11, NLT). For when we hold a grudge, although we didn't mean to, we allow the devil to walk right in. Do not give him that opportunity!

There are basically two kinds of hurts: (1) when people do not intend to hurt us—they don't know they have done it, and (2) when people are deliberately unkind—they surely know they have hurt us. And yet, strange as it may seem, most people you will have to forgive don't even think they have done anything wrong! That hurts even more. What do you do then? You still forgive them. As I advised in an earlier chapter, *don't* go to them and say, "You might like to know I have forgiven you." I can safely guarantee you will start World War III in a split second. Furthermore, when we tell people we have forgiven them, chances are we haven't! We only want to make sure they know how hurt we have been. We can't bear the thought that they don't know what they have done to us. But Jesus said, "Father, forgive them, for they do not know what they are doing" (Luke 23:34). Make Jesus your model.

Our Salvation Is Not the Issue

It must be repeated, as I stated in chapter 8, that forgiving others is not a condition for salvation; nor is the issue of whether we will or will not go to heaven even implied. When Jesus warns that we will not be forgiven unless we forgive, it might be thought by some sincere people that He was making our forgiving others a condition of our salvation. No. Thank God this is *not* the case. If it were, nobody would be saved. And yet to assert, as some do, that not forgiving others means we either cannot be saved or that we could lose our salvation—which is equally sad—is to miss the entire point of Jesus' teaching on the kingdom of God.

I say it again: if my forgiving others, as God requires, is a condition of my being righteous before God and therefore knowing whether I will go to heaven when I die, I would have no hope whatever of being a Christian.

I am ashamed to admit it, but I myself did not come into this teaching of total forgiveness until several years after I became the minister of Westminster Chapel. I was converted when I was six years old, called to preach when I was nineteen, pastor of a church at twenty, and later went to university and seminary. I had been in the ministry for over twenty-five years when I began to forgive people who hurt me.

If forgiveness was a condition of my salvation, it means I was not saved until years after I became the minister of Westminster Chapel! I do not believe that for a second. It would also mean that if I slipped (which I have done) and momentarily judged another or felt angry toward someone who hurt me, then—for a moment—I was lost, but got saved again when I came to myself and forgave my enemy and stopped judging. What kind of Christianity is that? A person who lives like that would be a nervous wreck day and night! That also would mean that salvation is earned by sheer good works. But that is not New Testament teaching.

Forgiving others is not only a good work, it is probably the most noble, admirable, and satisfying work one can achieve on this earth. And if such a work is what prepares us for heaven, then Jesus' teaching flies in the face of what Paul taught. He said, "For it is by grace you have been saved, through faith—and this is not from yourselves, it is the gift of God—*not by works*, so that no one can boast" (Eph. 2:8–9, emphasis mine). Paul went on to say that we are God's "workmanship, created in Christ Jesus for good works" (v. 10, ESV). It is being saved that *enables* us to do good works, such as totally forgiving our enemies. But what God enables us to do—forgive our enemies—is not what He stipulates in order to be saved.

Furthermore, believe me, total forgiveness is a life sentence—a life commitment—and something we must work on as long as we live.

Why Should We Totally Forgive?

What, then, is the reason for Jesus' teaching on forgiveness? It is to inherit His *conscious and enabling presence*, which is what He means by "the kingdom" in the Sermon on the Mount. Those who are offered the kingdom are those who are *already* followers of Jesus. When Jesus said, "Ask and it will be given to you; seek and you will find; knock and the door will be opened to you" (Matt. 7:7), it was directed to those who had not only heard all He taught regarding the kingdom, but who wanted all of God they could have. Jesus' teaching makes us hungry for God! When we read what He has to say in the Sermon on the Mount, our hearts should *burn within us* that we could experience such a relationship with the Father.

What is required for such a relationship? Total forgiveness. All that Jesus taught about being merciful and blessing our enemies was not idle talk; neither was it merely putting forth lofty principles that we admire. No. His teaching is to be applied by those who have already been saved, whose justification is by faith alone; it is they—not the lost—who are called to total forgiveness.

So what does it mean that our heavenly Father will also forgive us if we forgive those who sin against us? It means we can enjoy intimacy with Him here below—His immediate, direct, and conscious manifest presence. Total forgiveness, ridding us of poisonous bitterness, opens the door to knowing the Father so that God is as *real* to us as the air we breathe and as real as seeing the world He has made. Real. Yes, God is real. It is what the disciples experienced on the day of Pentecost. The person of Jesus was as real to them by the Spirit as He had been previously to them when they saw Him in the flesh. John talked about what they had "seen with our eyes, which we have looked at and our hands have touched"—namely, Jesus. The very fellowship with the Father that John was describing makes Jesus as real as if He were there before our eyes (1 John 1:1).

In a word: total forgiveness brings the anointing of the Holy Spirit; bitterness keeps Him away. Therefore the way we know we have forgiven is the immediate sense of God's presence. You are given this when you forgive; you lose this when you do not. You do not lose your salvation, but you do indeed forfeit—even if only temporarily—the anointing of the Spirit and the sense of His presence.

The Holy Spirit Depicted as a Dove

Paul talked about grieving the Holy Spirit, which we do chiefly by bitterness. But when we grieve the Spirit we do not lose our salvation; after all, he said, "Do not grieve the Holy Spirit of God, with whom you were sealed for the day of redemption" (Eph. 4:30). Nothing can be clearer than that! But when we grieve the Spirit by not totally forgiving our enemies, the anointing lifts from us; He does not "remain," He does not stay. The dove came down on Jesus and *remained* on Him (John 1:32–33). I wish He would remain on me! But I admit to grieving Him, which causes the dove to lift and fly away for a while. Total forgiveness attracts the dove so that He comes down on us; bitterness chases Him away.

This is the meaning of Jesus' words, "For if you forgive other people when they sin against you, your heavenly Father will also forgive you. But if you do not forgive others their sins, your Father will not forgive your sins" (Matt. 6:14–15)—that is, as long as you are in a state of not forgiving others. But once you confess your sins (1 John 1:9) and turn from them so as to reject all "bitterness, rage and anger" and begin "forgiving each other, just as in Christ God forgave you" (Eph. 4:31–32), the dove comes down and you have the witness of the Father's forgiveness. And by the way, He won't bend the rules for any of us—for you, the high-profile Christian leader, the aged saint, the most talented minister, or me.

The dove is a very sensitive, shy bird. This is apparently

why the Holy Spirit is depicted as a dove in the New Testament. And yet the Holy Spirit is far more sensitive than a dove! We must learn to know God's ways, which Israel failed to do (Heb. 3:7–11), so that we can sense when the dove lifts from us. Bitterness chases the dove away; total forgiveness—and nothing less—brings Him back. I'm sorry, but that is the way it is.

Refusing to Punish

Forgiving your enemy—or whoever has hurt you—means *refusing to punish them*. Perfect love casts out fear, and fear has to do with punishment (1 John 4:18). When we don't forgive, fear creeps in; we want those people we haven't forgiven to be afraid of us! We want to punish them by making them afraid. When the brothers of Joseph discovered that the prime minister of Egypt was actually Joseph (whom they had hoped never to see again), they were "terrified." But Joseph said to them, "Come close to me." The last thing he wanted was for his brothers to fear him (Gen. 45:3–4).

You must refuse to punish the one who has been unjust and has sinned against you by not damaging their credibility. We must resist damaging their reputation because of what they did to us. That is what I wanted to do—damage the influence of those who had been unfair toward me. But God said, *No! Stop it!* I had to keep quiet about it and tell nobody. It was hard. So hard. But a major part of total forgiveness is never telling anyone how you have been hurt. Yes, you may need to tell *one other person* for therapeutic reasons. But only one. And then, of course, you must tell God. He knows. Let the knowledge that *Jesus knows* be your peace and joy. And when you slip and forfeit God's presence for a while, return to Him; He will return to you. The dove will come down and reside with you. I promise it.

I suppose the hardest thing of all is to pray that God will bless them. One day I found myself saying, "Lord, bless them," but only because I knew it was the right thing to do. And then, as if the Lord intervened and had a conversation with me: "And what if I *really do* bless them, RT?"

I said, "Lord, You wouldn't do *that*, would You?"

But that is the point! When you pray for your enemy, you don't merely say, "Lord, I commit them to You." That's not good enough. That's a cop-out. You are probably still hoping that God will punish them! It isn't easy, but when you really do pray for God to bless your enemy—and truly mean it—you cross over into the supernatural and experience how real God is.

But how can you be motivated to do this? The way forward for wanting to experience God's forgiveness in this regard is when you prize fellowship with the Father, desire pleasing Him, and cherish the anointing of the Spirit above all else.

The Consequence of Unforgiveness

And yet it is most sobering to read, "But if you do not forgive others their sins, your Father will not forgive your sins" (Matt. 6:15). This is scary. Although Jesus does not mean I will go to hell, there is a danger of crossing over a line so that I forfeit such intimacy for a long time—perhaps forever. It is serious, serious business not to forgive. I have watched lives torn to shreds because of bitterness. I have not only seen marriages irretrievably broken down and destroyed, I have watched those who once knew the joy of the Lord in their lives fall into bitterness from which they were never to be extricated. I have watched them grow old and cold; I have seen them spend the rest of their lives preoccupied with their hurt and injustice, sometimes talking about nothing else. I have watched those I admired go to their graves with this bondage.

What does it mean at the judgment seat of Christ for those Christians who have not forgiven others who have sinned against them? They will "suffer loss"—which means loss of reward, or rejection for the prize they could have had. Yet they will "be saved—even though only as one escaping through the flames" ("saved…so as by fire," 1 Cor. 3:15, KJV). A reward at the judgment seat of Christ was very important to Paul. He said he made his body his slave in order that he not be rejected for the prize (1 Cor. 9:27).

Needlessly forfeiting your reward—is that what you want? Do you want to forfeit God's "well done"? It is promised only to those who have made every effort to add to their faith goodness; to goodness, knowledge; to knowledge, self-control; to self-control, perseverance; to perseverance, godliness; to godliness, brotherly kindness; and to brotherly kindness, love. Those who possess these qualities will be productive in the knowledge of our Lord Jesus Christ *and* will receive "a rich welcome into the eternal kingdom" (2 Pet. 1:5–11, "brotherly kindness" is used in the KJV).

Why does God hate an unforgiving spirit? It shows indifference to the greatest thing God ever did—namely, sending His Son to die on a cross for our sins. To be forgiven of all our sins is the most wonderful thing that can happen to us between the date of our birth and the time of our departure from this life. God forgiving us all our sins is what we most certainly don't deserve. But when we are forgiven, God wants us to be truly thankful and pass this knowledge to others—by our verbal witness and by our transparent love. When I have been forgiven but then point the finger at you, God says, "Stop! This will not do." It is a sober word: "Do not judge, or you too will be judged" (Matt. 7:1).

And yet total forgiveness is not necessarily reconciliation. It takes two to reconcile; it takes only one to forgive. The person you forgive may not want to be reconciled to you. What is more, you may not want to be reconciled to the person you forgive! It is not always good for a relationship to continue. If someone sleeps with your spouse, you forgive them; but you would not go on vacation with them. If a person has been a child molester, you forgive him; but you don't let him teach young children in your church. The main thing is not reconciliation but total forgiveness in your heart.

Inheriting the Blessing

The greater the suffering, the greater the anointing. The greater their injustice to you, the greater blessing that is promised to you. So if you have suffered more than others— or, let us say, more than anyone—instead of feeling sorry for yourself, feel congratulated! You have a promise of blessing, anointing, the conscious presence of God that will be greater than what is given to those around you who have not had to suffer what you have had to suffer, and have not had to forgive what you have had to forgive. All things work together for good to those who love God (Rom. 8:28), but you will postpone seeing things work together for good until you show you truly love God. You show you love Him by refusing to punish those who have hurt you but instead forgive them—totally.

Unforgiveness shows ingratitude to God for what He has done for you. God loves gratitude; He hates ingratitude. When you don't forgive after God has forgiven you, it shows ingratitude. God doesn't like that—not one bit. Show your gratitude to God by forgiving others as He has forgiven you!

A minister in Northern Ireland asked me a question I had not heard before: "Can your enemy be your wife?" I looked at him, smiled, and said, "Yes." He looked at me and said, "Thank you." Yes, your spouse can be like an enemy. The message of total forgiveness can save most marriages. But it takes two to reconcile. The main thing is that you yourself totally forgive what your spouse has done, that there is no pointing of the finger, no keeping a record of wrongs (1 Cor. 13:5). Your own marriage could be saved by sundown today if both of you would stop pointing the finger. And if your spouse continues to point the finger at you, you be the magnanimous one and stop it at once. The blessing of the Holy Spirit should be too important to you that you get your way in everything. After all, love "does not insist on its own way" (1 Cor. 13:5, ESV).

The characteristics of an unforgiving spirit are resentment, keeping a record of wrongs, telling people what "they" did to you, and living for revenge. Resentment chases the dove away. Keeping a record of wrongs forfeits the immediate sense of God's presence. Living for revenge forces God to hide His face from us until we make the choice to forgive them—totally.

An Act of the Will

Total forgiveness is a choice. Yes, you have to make a choice. It is an act of the will. Caution: don't wait until you feel "led." I meet few people who ever feel "led" to forgive. They feel "led" to hold a grudge, because holding a grudge is the natural thing to do; it always seems so right at the time. The only time you will probably feel led to forgive is when God stops you and speaks to you. Possibly like right now. If God is dealing with you as you read these lines, put this book down, ask Him to forgive you for your unforgiveness—and forgive them. Make the choice—now.

Here is a prayer I recommend you pray. If you can pray this from your heart, you will be on your way toward enjoying more of the kingdom Jesus preached about and fulfilling God's will for your life regarding forgiveness:

> Lord Jesus Christ, I need You. I want You. I am sorry for my sins. I am sorry for my unforgiveness. Wash away my sins by Your blood. I welcome Your Holy Spirit. I forgive them. You forgive them. I will not tell what they did. I will not let them be afraid of me. I will not make them feel guilty. I will let them save face. I accept that I will have to do this again and again, that this is a life sentence. I bless them. You bless them. I set them free. Thank You for Your patience with me. Amen.

If you truly meant that, you will never be the same again—unless you go back on what you have prayed. Yes, pray it again and again. God knows you struggle with this. God knows this could be major in your life. It was so major that Jesus returned to this issue after giving us the Lord's Prayer. But you will be so glad He did. This is what sets you free.

As total forgiveness is a choice, so too is an unforgiving spirit. When you hold a grudge you are making a choice; you choose *not* to let them off the hook. I'm afraid it also shows you are not sufficiently grateful that God has forgiven you. Show that you are grateful to God by totally forgiving them. You will also demonstrate you are the very kind of "workmanship" God has created for His glory (Eph. 2:10, ESV).

God Does Not Cease to Be Our Father

And did you notice the words "your Father" in Matthew 6:14–15? Twice in these verses are the words "your heavenly Father" and "your Father." "Your Father will not forgive your sins." Why? It is because God does not cease to be your Father. Nothing changes that relationship. He never ceases to be our Father—even when we don't forgive people who have sinned against us. It grieves Him; it disappoints Him; it hurts Him. But He is still our Father. He may chasten us. After all, whom the Lord loves He disciplines, chastens (Heb. 12:6). He will do what He must to get our attention.

Finally, what is the real reason that Jesus adds this P.S. to the Lord's Prayer? I believe it is to motivate us to forgive, to keep us from unnecessary chastening and not inheriting the kingdom. This verse is a warning. We all need it. It is because we are loved *so much* that God speaks as He does.

My loving counsel as I bring this book to a close: forgive them. It is the greatest freedom on earth. Where the Spirit of the Lord is—and works in us ungrieved—there is liberty (2 Cor. 3:17, KJV). Don't come short of that liberty. Set them free, and you will be free. Bless them, and you will be blessed. Forgive them, and you will be forgiven. The anointing, freedom, joy, and blessing that will come upon your life as a consequence is infinitely greater than the fleshly wish for vengeance.

Conclusion

You may not have expected that this book on the Lord's Prayer should end with a caution about totally forgiving those who have sinned against you. But this is the way Jesus Himself, who introduced this extraordinary prayer, chose to wrap it up. I do so too.

One last suggestion: you might want to go back and read this book again. If you do so having totally forgiven those who have hurt you, I can safely promise that you will enjoy this book twice as much—right from the start.

May the blessing of God Almighty—Father, Son, and Holy Spirit—be upon you afresh from this moment. Amen.

NOTES

Foreword

1. E. M. Bounds, *The Complete Works of E. M. Bounds on Prayer* (Grand Rapids, MI: Baker Books, 1990), 299.

Chapter 1

1. Blue Letter Bible, s.v. "*kakos*," accessed January 5, 2023, https://www.blueletterbible.org/lexicon/g2556/kjv/tr/0-1/.
2. Britannica, s.v. "Shema," accessed January 5, 2023, https://www.britannica.com/topic/Shema.
3. David Martyn Lloyd-Jones, *Studies in the Sermon on the Mount* (Grand Rapids, MI: 1971), 325.
4. George P. Wood, "Your Father Knows What You Need," *Influence*, January 12, 2018, https://influencemagazine.com/practice/your-father-knows-what-you-need.
5. John Calvin, Grace Quotes, accessed October 6, 2022, https://gracequotes.org/quote/believers-do-not-pray-with-the-view-of-informing-god-about-things-unknown-to-him-or-of-exciting-him-to-do-his-duty-or-of-urging-him-as-though-he-were-reluctant-on-the-contrary-they-pray-in-order-t/.
6. John Wesley, Quote Fancy, accessed October 6, 2022, https://quotefancy.com/quote/1464531/John-Wesley-God-does-nothing-except-in-response-to-believing-prayer.
7. "William Temple," AZ Quotes, accessed January 5, 2023, https://www.azquotes.com/quote/1307216.

Chapter 2

1. James Lau, "When You Pray by Martyn Lloyd Jones," *My Inward Journey*, jameslau88.com, May 20, 2022, https://jameslau88.com/2020/05/20/when-you-pray-by-martyn-lloyd-jones/.
2. Lloyd-Jones, *Studies in the Sermon on the Mount*, 328.
3. "What Does the Greek Word 'Tetelestai' Mean?" Bible.org, accessed January 5, 2023, https://bible.org/question/what-does-greek-word-tetelestai-mean.

Chapter 3

1. Walter C. Smith, "Immortal, Invisible, God Only Wise," Hymnary.org, accessed October 10, 2022, https://hymnary.org/text/immortal_invisible_god_only_wise.

Chapter 4

1. Bible Study Tools, s.v. "*hagiazo*," accessed October 11, 2022, https://www.biblestudytools.com/lexicons/greek/nas/hagiazo.html.
2. William Shakespeare, "'A Rose by Any Other Name,' Meaning & Context," No Sweat Shakespeare, accessed October 11, 2022, https://nosweatshakespeare.com/quotes/famous/rose-by-any-other-name.

Chapter 6

1. Blue Letter Bible, s.v. "*doxa*," accessed October 13, 2022, https://www.blueletterbible.org/lexicon/g1391/kjv/tr/0-1.
2. George Keith and R. Keen, "How Firm a Foundation, Ye Saints of the Lord," Hymnary.org, accessed October 13, 2022, https://hymnary.org/text/how_firm_a_foundation_ye_saints_of.

3. Margaret J. Harris, "I Will Praise Him," Hymnary.org, accessed October 13, 2022, https://hymnary.org/text/when_i_saw_the_cleansing_fountain.

Chapter 8

1. Bible Study Tools, s.v. *"opheilema,"* accessed December 8, 2022, https://www.biblestudytools.com/lexicons/greek/nas/opheilema.html.
2. Blue Letter Bible, s.v. *"hamartia,"* accessed December 8, 2022, https://www.blueletterbible.org/lexicon/g266/kjv/tr/0-1.
3. Blue Letter Bible, s.v. *"aphiemi,"* accessed January 5, 2023, https://www.blueletterbible.org/lexicon/g863/kjv/tr/0-1/
4. "The Lord's Prayer" (traditional), The (Online) Book of Common Prayer, accessed December 8, 2022, https://www.bcponline.org/General/paternoster.html.

Chapter 9

1. C. F. D. Moule, "Unsolved Problem in the Temptation-Clause in the Lord's Prayer," *Reformed Theological Review* 33 (September–December 1974): 65-75.
2. Bible Study Tools, s.v. *"peirasmos,"* accessed December 12, 2022, https://www.biblestudytools.com/lexicons/greek/nas/peirasmos.html#:~:text=pi%2Dras%2Dmos',the%20Galatians%20toward%20Paul%20(Gal.
3. Frances Ridley Havergal, "Like a River, Glorious," Hymnal.net, accessed December 13, 2022, https://www.hymnal.net/en/hymn/h/719.

Chapter 10

1. SermonIndex.net, s.v. *"poneros"* (*ponerou*), accessed December 13, 2022, https://www.sermonindex.net/modules/articles/index.php?view=article&aid=33996.
2. Martin Luther, "A Mighty Fortress," Hymnary.org, accessed December 15, 2022, https://hymnary.org/text/a_mighty_fortress_is_our_god_a_bulwark.

Chapter 11

1. St. Anselm, "Ontological Argument," as cited in *Proslogion*, Britannica, accessed December 15, 2022, https://www.britannica.com/topic/ontological-argument.
2. Bible Study Tools, s.v. *"dunamis,"* accessed December 15, 2022, https://www.biblestudytools.com/lexicons/greek/nas/dunamis.html.
3. Bible Study Tools, s.v. *"exousia,"* accessed December 15, 2022, https://www.biblestudytools.com/lexicons/greek/nas/exousia.html.
4. Blue Letter Bible, s.v. *"kabod,"* accessed December 16, 2022, https://www.blueletterbible.org/lexicon/h3519/kjv/wlc/0-1/.
5. Blue Letter Bible, s.v. *"doxa,"* accessed December 16, 2022, https://www.blueletterbible.org/lexicon/g1391/kjv/tr/0-1/.
6. Bible Study Tools, s.v. "amen," accessed December 16, 2022, https://www.biblestudytools.com/dictionary/amen/.

Chapter 12

1. Bible Study Tools, s.v. *"ean,"* accessed December 16, 2022, https://www.biblestudytools.com/lexicons/greek/nas/ean.html; Blue Letter Bible, s.v. *"gar,"* accessed December 16, 2022, https://www.blueletterbible.org/lexicon/g1063/kjv/tr/0-1/.

ABOUT THE AUTHOR

D R. R. T. Kendall was born in Ashland, Kentucky, on
July 13, 1935. He has been married to Louise for more
than fifty years. They have two children, a son (Robert
Tillman II, married to Annette) and a daughter (Melissa),
and one grandson (Tobias Robert Stephen).

Dr. Kendall is a graduate of Trevecca Nazarene University
(AB), Southern Baptist Theological Seminary (MDiv),
University of Louisville (MA), and Oxford University
(DPhil *Oxon.*). His doctoral thesis was published by Oxford
University Press under the title *Calvin and English Calvinism
to 1647.* He was awarded the Doctor of Divinity by Trevecca
Nazarene University in 2008.

Before he and his family went to England, Dr. Kendall
pastored churches in Palmer, Tennessee; Carlisle, Ohio; Fort
Lauderdale, Florida; and Salem, Indiana. He was pastor of
Calvary Baptist Church in Lower Heyford, Oxfordshire, UK
(paralleling his three years at Oxford). He became the minister of Westminster Chapel on February 1, 1977, and was
there for exactly twenty-five years, succeeding G. Campbell
Morgan and D. Martyn Lloyd-Jones. He retired on February
1, 2002. His twenty-five years at Westminster Chapel are
the subject of his book *In Pursuit of His Glory.*

Shortly after Dr. Kendall's retirement, he became involved
in the Alexandria Peace Process, founded by Lord Carey,
former archbishop of Canterbury, and Canon Andrew

White, the archbishop's envoy to the Middle East. From this came a special relationship with the late Yasser Arafat, president of the Palestinian National Authority, and Rabbi David Rosen, Israel's most distinguished orthodox Jewish rabbi. Dr. Kendall and Rabbi Rosen wrote a book together, *The Christian and the Pharisee*.

Dr. Kendall is the author of more than fifty books, including *Total Forgiveness, Double Anointing, We've Never Been This Way Before, The Parables of Jesus, God Meant It for Good*, and *Did You Think to Pray?* He has an international ministry and spends his time preaching and writing. He and Louise live in Hendersonville, Tennessee, where he fishes occasionally.